Praise F

The seed of devotion begins with a time when you feel seen and loved unconditionally. That's the gift of the true teacher or guru. That seed is nourished by our practice, and by cultivating that depth of love in every moment of our life. In *A Lotus on Fire*, Vickie reveals the tender and devotional love that was ignited in one moment of awakening with Vietnamese Zen Master Thich Nhat Hanh, and how that love slowly expands to embrace the whole world.

Deva Premal and Miten, Grammy-nominated mantra singers and devotional musicians

In *A Lotus on Fire*, Vickie MacArthur invites us into her expanding heart. An unexpected meeting with Zen Master Thich Nhat Hanh brought her face to face with love, vulnerability, and compassion. Vickie invites us all to consider how merging the practices of Christian love and Zen insight might expand our own hearts.

Jonathan Prescott, Clinical Chaplain and Pastoral Counselor, Ordained student of Zen Master Thich Nhat Hanh, Founder of Wise Caregiving

A Lotus on Fire is a sensitive portrayal of one woman's spiritual quest, passing through the inevitable sufferings that life entails, and in the course of which the author's heart is broken open to the universal spirit, which is love.

Antoinette Voûte Roeder, Author of *The Space Between* and *Poems for Meditation*

In *A Lotus on Fire*, Vickie offers us rich and vulnerable prose on how she brought her kensho, a moment of enlightenment, into her family, her community, and her life. Joseph Campbell describes this as the journey of the hero, how we come down from the mountain and integrate this into our life. Vickie reminds us that it is not the seeing of God that is important, but the doing and the being of the presence of love in the world. Lovingly and skillfully, Vickie braids the teachings and practices of yoga, Christianity, and Buddhism into a seamless story of inter-being for all. She is a wise guide to the great mystery, and how to live authentically in the world with a heart undisturbed, dwelling in peace, amidst the inevitable ups and downs of life.

Dr. Peggy Rowe Ward, Senior Dharma Teacher in the tradition of Thich Nhat Hanh, Co-author of *Making Friends with Time* and *Love's Garden*

Vickie MacArthur's prose takes us gently by the hand on an intense and intimate journey into her spiritual connection with "Thay," the Vietnamese monk, Thich Nhat Hanh, a world-renowned Buddhist teacher. From Canada to California and France, Vickie delves into how one moment of looking into Thay's compassionate eyes awakened her soul to a love beyond boundaries of culture and religion. Written as personal letters to her teacher, Vickie's memoir reveals the depth of her inner journey, from a grieving daughter to a woman kindled by transformative love.

Rev. Dr. Teresa Elder Hanlon, Spiritual director, retreat facilitator, and priest with RCWP Canada

Vickie MacArthur insightfully pens her holy yearning for union with the Divine through letters to her teacher Thich Nhat Hanh. In so doing, she elevates letter-writing into sacred discipleship. Vickie articulates the sanctity of mysticism as an ongoing conversation between disciple and teacher, an interbeing between Thay and the Christ, and peace between Buddhism and Christianity. In *A Lotus on Fire*, Vickie bravely reveals the mystery of embodied communion. She beckons the reader to consider their capacity for listening, claiming, and naming personal conversations with all that may be known as Sacred.

Lana Cullis. Writer, teacher, and friend

A Lotus on Fire

How a Buddhist Monk Ignited My Heart

Vickie MacArthur

Cover and interior design by Beate Wichmann.

Cover image: Dreamstime

Author photo: Jaime Vedres

ISBN 978-1-7387815-1-5

To Thay,

Living Buddha, Living Christ
The One Love living in all hearts
Eternal flame

Contents

Foreword

FOR A MOMENT IT OCCURRED TO ME that I could write this foreword as a letter addressing Vickie's beloved Thay, the late Buddhist mystic and teacher, Thich Nhat Hanh. The affectionate ease with which she writes letters to him on matters of the deepest significance in her life left me imagining the ease I might experience in taking up my own letter-writing pen. This spiritual memoir, written as letters from Vickie to her mentor, will be a gift for all those who, in this time of spiritual fluidity, seek encouragement and inspiration in addressing the kind of critical spiritual issues that Vickie brings before us.

I'm thinking especially of large numbers of folks who were, until very recently, occupants of pews in traditional places of Christian worship, who grew up, as Vickie says, "with stories and teachings of Jesus" that are no longer persuasive when it comes to holding membership in these communities of faith. The story of Vickie's encounters with Thay speaks to us of "an embodied experience of the Living Buddha, Living Christ." Now when Vickie reads the bible and other sacred scriptures, "the words come alive" for her. The personal testimony she offers in these letters to Thay could, indeed, be "words come alive" for folks who are yearning to be addressed by spirit-centred testimony. Whether within or without the traditional bounds of religion, readers find in Vickie's letters sacred accompaniment in bringing meaning as they, too, address the intimate realities of their own lives.

I met Vickie in the context of the Pacific Jubilee Program (PJP)*, which has as its primary focus the training of people in the art of spiritual accompaniment. In the course of that two-year deepening in contemplative practice, we focused for much of the time on the practice of presence, surrendering our society's value for advice-giving and problem-solving, and developing the capacity to listen deeply to the sacred in all things as we contracted with mystery and gave fresh attention to silence. Over the past decade of my involvement in PJP, I've become ever more attentive to the places where I perceive accompaniment to be creatively at work in relationships. This book is a remarkable, if unconventional, witness to the power of accompaniment. In the story of Vickie's unfolding relationship with her spiritual mentor, Thay's accompanying presence is transformative. Indeed, as I take a moment now to recall the Seven Key Words of the Jubilee Program, I can see a lovely confluence between them and what has come to life in her journey with Thich Nhat Hanh. Her narrative is one of yearning for the *contemplative* life. Her writing is in every sentence *evocative* and *spacious*. In Vickie's attention to the present moment and all that it holds, we see her valuing that which is *embodied*, *integrative*, and *experiential*. And what is this book about if not the *transformative* journey?

As I seek to find words to do justice to the integrity of Vickie's story, I am aware of the pleasure I felt in reading this book. As one who is drawn to poetry and poetic language, I delight in clear and evocative writing. In this moment I turn, quite arbitrarily, to a page in the text, and give myself again to the beauty of Vickie's writing:

Then, sometimes with just one breath, that striving person dissolves, and there is just the gentle breeze brushing my skin, the eagle soaring in the vast blue sky above. Time flows effortlessly, without my trying to control it. I can be myself. I can allow others to be themselves. I can let go of trying to attain something in the future. I can let go of the planning. I can let go of all the preconceived notions I have about my spiritual path or enlightenment. I can look into my teacher's eyes and

see myself perfectly reflected there. I already know the better
way to live alone. I just need to keep remembering, and loving
the part of me that forgets.

See what I mean?

Gratitude to Vickie for taking the time to craft the words to honour
her journey with the gentle Buddhist monk who ignited love in her
heart. May that evocation be yours also as you give your contemplative
attention to this transforming text. Blessed be.

TIM SCORER
August 2022

Tim Scorer is a retreat leader who focuses on matters of spiritual
accompaniment, contemplative practice, spiritual eldering, and
poetry. All of that is wrapped up in a very full life as grandparent,
life-partner, gardener and traveler, on Bowen Island, BC.

---

* Pacific Jubilee is the west coast offering of the Canadian Jubilee Program for training
in the art of spiritual direction and accompaniment.
www.canadianjubilee.ca/pacific-programs

Gratitude

Writing, to me, is very much like meditation and prayer—often starting as a solitary practice that is then sustained and enlivened with the support of a good community. This book started out in the privacy of my own journals as "Letters to Thay," a way to plumb the depths of the deeply transformative experience of awakening I had with Thich Nhat Hanh. Slowly, as this spiritual love story began to unfold into a living, breathing manuscript, I realized it would take both discernment and courage to free the words from the privacy of my journals and the vulnerability of my heart. I needed the sanctuary of sangha, a community that could believe in me, encourage me, challenge me, hold me through life's ups and downs (including a devastating accident), and finally integrate the collective wisdom of our shared gifts, passion and understanding. Indeed, it takes a village!

With deep gratitude:

To Thay, for your gaze of Divine love that ignited the spark of awakening, becoming the flame of love and inspiration for this book. To look into your eyes has been one of the greatest blessings of my life. May this book be another testament to your life of selfless service and love for Mother Earth and all beings, and for the pure transmission and realization of love. You are the Living Buddha, Living Christ. I walk for you. I breathe for you. I carry this Love and Light wherever I go.

To all the monks and nuns, and dharma teachers, and students of Thich Nhat Hanh around the world, thank you for your tireless devotion to sharing the dharma and practices that can heal and transform not only our individual lives, but the world. Your stories of Thay and his teachings have nourished and inspired me, and given me the courage to share my own story. Our stories inter-are.

To Susan Scott, my editor, midwife, and mentor, for your fierce and passionate belief in the power of spiritual life writing to change and transform our world. It is rare to find an editor who feels like a soul mate, someone with shared spiritual roots, who understands the underlying essence of what we want to say before we even put it into words, who can then help shape, cut, snip, and finally weave our thoughts all together to reflect both the reality of life and the radiance of Spirit. You are a wise and compassionate soul, who helps bring out the "wise woman" in me.

To all the other professionals who have been part of the ever-evolving process of giving this book life and depth: Elizabeth McLachlan, my very first editor, who read the first part of the manuscript, quickly dispensing with the wordy introduction, and helping me to "write my way into the story." To Mark Matousek, for your guidance and practice of "Writing To Awaken," asking the questions beneath the questions, challenging me to "find my clay feet" and reveal the vulnerability beneath the veneer of spirituality. To Beate Wichmann, artist and graphic designer, for a cover and book design that brings the story to life! To Joy Thierry Llewellyn, fellow traveler and Indie writer, for your patience in helping me navigate the confusing world of publishing and distribution.

To my dear friend Lanette: ever since first sharing maternity clothes, our lives and families have been woven together in both joy and sorrow. Thank you for allowing me to share part of Coley's story, as seen and felt through my own experience, knowing this is only a small reflection of her life and indomitable spirit. Like Coley, may we all learn to recognize "small moments of grace," even in the face of great pain and suffering.

To Lana, dear friend and writing sister: what a delight to discover, in the midst of our lifelong friendship, our shared love for writing and sharing these kinds of spiritual life stories. These last few years have been such a rich and revelatory journey, as we both have faced health challenges that could have stopped us in our tracks, but instead have cracked us open and strengthened our resolve. We never know where our stories will lead, but I couldn't have finished this book without your love and support in my darkest hours of uncertainty and doubt.

To Tim Scorer, lover of poetry and writing that "shimmers." Thank you for helping me see the poet in my own soul, and for writing the foreword for this book. It is an invitation to the kind of deep listening and communion that takes place in spiritual companioning, and the listening space beyond words. Thanks to all my mentors, companions and friends at Pacific Jubilee, as we accompanied each other on a two-year pilgrimage and training program. You created sanctuary for me to listen, to write, and to express the yearnings of my soul.

To my spiritual companions: Teresa Hanlon, for your holy listening, and healing prayer, and for always finding just the right poem or scripture that speaks to my heart. Thank you for receiving all my innermost stories of Thay with unconditional love and understanding, allowing me to fully claim and catch the "glimmers" of insight, so they could flow to others through my own life and writing. To Peggy Rowe Ward, for your Buddhist, Christian, Bhakti, devotional heart that attuned to the fire in my own heart, for embodied practices of yoga and breath that helped heal and release the trauma from my accident, and for our shared love for Thay that expresses the kind of inter-spiritual love so needed in our world today. To Jonathan Prescott, for our rich conversations around spiritual friends and "one practice in two bodies," and for your deep devotion to Zen practice, and wise caregiving. To Antoinette Voûte-Roeder, for your poetry and love for Mother Earth, and encouragement to just write and be myself.

To Deva and Miten, your love for your own beloved teacher, and your music and mantras live and vibrate with love in my heart. I am so grateful to have met you many years ago at the Toronto Yoga

Show, then continue to sing and chant with you at workshops and concerts across Canada and at Blue Spirit in Costa Rica. Your music has given this book the notes and melody to "Fly High, Let the Earth Touch the Sky!"

My inter-spiritual heart allows me to flow with ease and grace through different spiritual communities. Through my parents and grandparents, I am rooted in the Community of Christ, and am grateful for the faith of many generations trickling through me. I have been spiritually formed and shaped by this Christian community that has nurtured a kind of faith that can expand beyond conventional religious boundaries.

I am also grateful for my network of Plum Village Buddhist sanghas: Dawning Light Sangha in Lethbridge, the Wild Rose Sangha in Calgary, Anacortes Mindfulness Community with Jonathan Prescott, the Lotus Institute with Peggy Rowe Ward and Larry Ward. All of these sanghas express Thay's vision for creating communities of support and practice all over the world. COVID-19 has helped erase some of the geographical boundaries and allowed more of us to practice together through online communities. This book would not be possible without that practice and support.

To my Spirit in Motion Yoga Community: for many years you have entrusted me with the sacred calling of teaching and sharing the practice of yoga with you. Yet teaching is never a one-way relationship. As Thay says, "Teacher and student are not separate." I have learned from and been inspired by my students in countless ways. I have learned from your questions. I have learned from your bodies. I have learned from your minds. Because of you, I know true courage. I have felt both the trust and vulnerability of your hearts. Your stories are inter-woven with mine.

With love and gratitude to my family, immediate and extended, for supporting me in both visible and invisible ways. To Brendan, for your willingness to dig deep beneath the surface, for reading my manuscript before it was finished, and for your "skateboarder" soul that is finding the rhythm amongst the rough and smooth edges of life. To Andrew, for allowing me to tell your story of healing, and for the diligent hard-working young man you've grown into. I always told you that miracles are meant to be shared. Your life is living proof. To Briana, for your Irish spunk and Italian passion, and for your care and sense of humour, as I recovered from my accident. You brighten our world.

Finally, to Doug, my love, my heart, my home. Thank you for loving me exactly as I am. Our love is real. Our love is timeless. It is because of already seeing the love reflected in your eyes, that I could receive the love in Thay's eyes, and reflect that love back to others. May we all see and be seen through this timeless gaze of Love.

Prologue

A Divine Love Affair

It has to be a passionate love affair with the Divine if you really want to get there.
Swami Sivananda Radha

This is the story of a moment of spiritual awakening that was really part of many moments of awakening. My secret love affair with Spirit began in a mystical relationship with Buddhist Master Thich Nhat Hanh (Thay) that ultimately pointed me back to the vast web of loving relationships we all are. This mystical love lives beneath the surface until something or someone touches the spark within us that ignites the flame that awakens our heart. May this book be that spark for you.

PART 1

Igniting the Flame

This awakened understanding is quicker than lightning,
quicker than the spark that comes from flint.
Thich Nhat Hanh,
Nothing To Do, Nowhere To Go

CHAPTER 1

Awakening the Heart

"AWAKENING THE HEART" RETREAT

WITH BUDDHIST MASTER THICH NHAT HANH.

AUGUST 8 – 13, 2011.

UNIVERSITY OF BRITISH COLUMBIA, VANCOUVER, CANADA

I Have Arrived, I Am Home

It's the first day of the "Awakening the Heart" retreat in Vancouver, and I am greeted by long line-ups of people slowly snaking towards a solid wall of registration tables. Suitcases and bags are scattered on the sidewalk and surrounding lawn, some neatly stacked, others set down carelessly, as if spit out of a baggage carousel at a busy airport. Setting my own over-packed suitcase down with a heavy sigh, I turn to see my girlfriend's car disappear around the corner. I resist the urge to run after her, and go back home. Lanette is likely returning to Canuck Place hospice, where her beautiful seventeen year-old daughter, Nicole (Coley), is in the final stages of a courageous fight with bone cancer. The cancer has metastasized and is draining the life from this once vibrant, smart, tree-loving girl.

How does one grieve this slow and pain-filled loss of one's own dear sweet child? I've spent the last three months at my mother's bedside in palliative care, watching as the tumour that began in her right ovary extinguished the spark in her blue eyes. Mother and daughter, daughter and mother, are forever intimately connected by the umbilical cord of life.

I look around only to realize that the people and noise and confusion are overwhelming. My heart is vulnerable and raw one month after my mother's death, and I have yet to adjust to being an orphan. Maybe one never does. With all these people milling about,

I feel the need to draw a protective shell around me. I signed up for this retreat back in February. Now, six months later, it seems like an eternity has passed. Ashley, my friend and fellow yoga teacher, had mentioned that Buddhist Monk, Thich Nhat Hanh, was offering a meditation retreat in Vancouver. I had read his book, *Living Buddha, Living Christ*, and loved the unique connections made between Buddhism and Christianity. I didn't know much else about him, but a small voice inside me nudged me to sign up for the retreat. With a few strokes of the keyboard, I found myself committed.

In March, my mother was diagnosed with Stage IV ovarian cancer. That same month, the earthquake that hit Japan created a tsunami that knocked out the nuclear reactors in Fukoshima. A burst pipe flooding our basement while my mother lay in her hospital bed seemed like a symbolic wave wiping out my own foundation, as I began to prepare for her impending death. The past five months have been a blur: doctor appointments, moving my mother out of her house and into palliative care, then keeping watch by her bedside as the cancer had its way with her. I've hardly thought about this retreat at all.

My heart feels exposed, yet for now it is covered by a protective bandage that has somehow allowed me to get through the past month of planning her funeral and dealing with the myriad details that surface amidst the grief of losing a loved one. I have attended many small yoga and meditation retreats before, but here I feel overwhelmed. Hundreds of people trying to register and settle at the same time doesn't seem at all conducive to meditation and the healing I had hoped to find.

A gentle breeze ruffles my hair, and I remember to breathe into this feeling of wanting to run away. This breath of fresh air reminds me that it is a miracle I'm able to be here at all. Life is always uncertain, yet that small voice I've always listened to reassures me that I'm exactly where I need to be, even with my vulnerable heart. So here I am, and here I will stay.

I settle back into the line-up. It takes an hour to reach the registration table, where at last I receive my registration package and room assignment. I am then directed to a small group, for a short introduction to the Plum Village mindfulness practices. A beautiful nun in brown robes and a brown headscarf teaches us the fine art of "stopping" and coming back to our breath every time we hear the bell. We practice a few steps of walking meditation, taking one slow step at a time. Meals are vegetarian, we are told, and will be in silence, to give us a chance to really taste our food. I find myself impatient and distracted. I think I already know how to be mindful. All I want to do is to find my room, unpack, and squeeze in a nap before supper. Finally, an overly cheerful volunteer shows me the way to the university residences. I discover that my room is on the third floor of an old dorm that has no elevator! After lugging my suitcase up six sets of stairs, I collapse on the small bed in what feels like a sauna (no air conditioning either!) Why am I here? What exactly am I looking for? I breathe, and trust that somehow the answer will come.

After supper, we all make our way to the other end of campus for the introductory dharma talk. The Thunderbird Gym, usually home to the sound of bouncing balls and whistles, pounding steps and echoing voices, has been converted into a large makeshift meditation hall. There is a small raised stage at the front. A single brown meditation cushion sits behind a podium, next to a simple arrangement of orchids. A large banner overhead announces the theme of the retreat, "Awakening the Heart," in Thay's calligraphic style. In front of the stage are row after row of meditation cushions, while at the back of the hall sit the chairs for those who need them. We wait for the revered Buddhist teacher to arrive. The room is alive with the hum of quiet voices. Monks and nuns with shaved heads and plain brown robes work peacefully and efficiently to ensure no detail is overlooked. Finally, a short bell sounds. We all stand, hands joined at our hearts, as the Zen Master Thich Nhat Hanh enters the hall with slow, measured steps. He stops beside the stage, bows and smiles, then motions for us to sit. The agile eighty-five year old monk sits down on the cushion, and effortlessly folds his legs beneath him.

He speaks about Avalokiteshvara, the Buddha of great compassion, and invites the monks and nuns to come up to chant. He instructs us to get in touch with our suffering, and allow it to be embraced by the energy of the sangha and by the Buddha. A nun playing a mournful melody on a violin is joined by a tall monk playing the cello, then the collective voices of the monastic choir all join in. I listen to the sound as I gently breathe into my own tender heart center. There are no tears, only a gentle softening of both my mind and body. That is enough for now.

The next morning begins with a guided meditation led by one of his monastics. "Breathing in, I know I am breathing in, breathing out I know I am breathing out. In....out....deep...slow." We all settle into the rhythm of our shared breath. I'm still a bit judgmental. These practices seem overly-simplified. Still, I begin to feel the energy of eight hundred people focused and breathing quietly together.

After a mostly silent vegetarian breakfast in the university cafeteria, we head to the meditation hall for a dharma talk. Thay talks about the first four practices of breathing. Thay has no notes and his words seem simple and easy to follow, although I sense there are many layers of understanding. His voice is soft. I have to listen carefully. Some terms are new to me. I jot down a few notes in my journal. As he talks, I realize that a few years ago I had picked up a book of his at a second-hand store. *The Sutra on the 16 Exercises of Breathing* is still sitting on my bookshelf, unopened. Books and teachers have a way of arriving at the right time in our lives.

After the talk, we go on walking meditation all together, a long, long line led by Thay and some monastics. We wind our way through the campus. Students stop and stare at this throng of people slowly walking past in silence. As we pass by the campus food court, I notice a Starbucks and consider breaking away for a quick latte.

This thought continues to grab my attention until we wind our way past the large clock tower and stop in a green space surrounded by trees. Thay sits down in the shade of a tree, and somehow we all find a place to sit in an expanding circle around him, while some take advantage of this photo opp to snap pictures of this revered teacher. I reach into my backpack to grab my own camera, but as I bring it up to focus, Thay turns around and looks directly at me. It's a penetrating look. Something makes me pause, and stop. In that moment, I realize I am treating this teacher as an object, and not as the respected living teacher he is. I slip my camera back into my bag, and settle into the silence and the melodious sounds of birds. I am simply present to what's right here, and now.

After lunch there is time for rest and relaxation before meeting later in the afternoon in small dharma family groups of about twenty people. This is a chance to connect and get to know others. It is a more personal space, where we are invited to share about our lives, and how we are doing with the practices. The nun who leads our group was ordained by Thay many years ago. Sister Thoai Nghiêm's depth of experience and wisdom show through her words and her quiet presence. She seems to hold us all peacefully, even in this sterile classroom.

The daily rhythm of the five-day retreat includes waking at 5 a.m. for meditation and chanting, breakfast, a dharma talk by Thay, followed by walking meditation, lunch, then rest, dharma family groups, then supper. Evenings, we are usually guided through different Plum Village practices. On the second evening, Sister Chân Không, who has been with Thay since his days in Vietnam, leads us in the practice of Deep Relaxation, and sings a lullaby in Vietnamese. I feel safe, like a baby held once more in my mother's arms. We also learn the practice of Touching the Earth, in reverence to our biological and spiritual ancestors. I think about my own parents and grandparents on both sides of my family. I am aware of many ministers and friends from my Christian roots, as well as the many teachers who have crossed my path on my journey into yoga and Eastern religions. I feel grateful to have had the opportunity and courage to move beyond the restrictive bonds of just one religion.

Despite the large retreat, the simple practices of just breathing and sitting and walking and listening begin to work their way under my skin and the protective layers around my heart. I find myself sinking into an inner space where I can begin to ride the roller coaster I've been on for the past five months at a much slower pace. Images and memories now arise as I let go of holding on so tight. Some images are clear and recognizable, like the outline of the North Shore Mountains etched against the clear blue sky on one of those rare sunny days here in Vancouver. Other memories are murky and dim, like the Gulf islands off the coast on a foggy day. I know the memories and feelings are there, they just won't quite come into focus. As my body relaxes, and my mind clears, memories and images of my mother's final five months begin to arise like helium balloons, free of the string tied to my heart: the doctor's kind face as she gave the cancer diagnosis, a bright cheery bouquet of green St. Paddy's Day balloons tied to my mother's hospital bed as she celebrated her 82nd birthday, quiet moments just sitting by the lake with her as she shared stories of both love and loss, watching her body fade away to a frail shadow of skin on bone, the raspy sound of her slow and laboured breathing, and the long pause before her last breath, as my husband and I held her hands.

I miss my mother. My eyes are moist, but there has been no great outpouring of uncontrollable grief, no torrent of tears. I find myself wondering if I am grieving properly, as if there are any maps or rules for grieving! While I sat with my mother in palliative care, I felt sadness for her suffering, but I was not overwhelmed. Am I repressing my feelings? Or have twenty-something years of simply showing up on my yoga mat and cushion every morning, along with the inevitable ups and downs of life, taught me about breathing and just being with my feelings as they come? Am I worrying too much?

Somehow just being at this retreat allows the edges of my thoughts to soften. I can dip beneath the surface to see what might be hiding there. For now, that is enough.

When the Student is Ready, the Teacher Appears

I always think that to be able to look into the eyes of one true Master is worth one hundred years studying his doctrine, his teaching. In him you have a direct example of enlightenment, of life...
Thich Nhat Hanh, *The Raft Is Not the Shore*

August 12
At today's dharma talk, people are invited up on stage to ask Thay "The Question of Your Heart," about their practice and life experience. "A good question does not have to be long," Thay says with twinkling eyes. "You can sit in that chair to ask your question," he says. "It's a beautiful view from up here." He points with a grin to a chair set directly across from where he sits. Surely he knows how much courage it takes to ask the question of your heart in front of eight hundred people!

Children seem to be welcome at Plum Village retreats and today, children are invited to ask their questions first, followed by teenagers and finally, adults. A pretty girl with dark hair pulled back in a ponytail bravely takes the chair in front of Thay. Her tiny bare feet dangle in the air. The meditation bell is sounded, then Thay's attendant hands her the microphone. "How did you feel when you left your country?" she asks. (In 1966, Thay was exiled from his home country of Vietnam for refusing to take sides, and for advocating for peace and an end of the hostilities there.)

I do not hear the answer. An inexplicable feeling washes over me, and I somehow find myself on my feet, as if compelled by some invisible force. I sidestep through the ocean of meditation cushions and find my way to the side of the stage, where a dozen others are lining up. I have no idea why I have gotten up, or what question I am going to ask. All I know is that my heart is beating wildly. Maybe I can hide out here, I think, until I can find my way back to my seat. But as I scout for an escape route, a monk gestures for all of us to come on stage. We are invited to sit on the floor around Thay while we wait our turn to ask our question. I hesitate, then follow the others.

Suddenly, I find myself sitting at the feet of the master, facing hundreds of onlookers. I still have no idea what I will say. I haven't really thought about the question of my heart. It's so fragile at the moment. I'm not sure what impelled me to get up in the first place. To make matters worse, I realize that I can't hear people's questions. The speakers are all turned towards the audience, while we sit off to one side. Finally, I remember to take a deep breath. My shoulders and face relax. My mind begins to clear a bit. I see the image of my mother's dear face, and feel her love in me. I feel the sadness of her passing. I miss her, but I know somehow that she lives on in me.

I sit still trying to stay mindful, thinking about my questions, watching my nervousness, observing my frustration at not being able to hear other people's questions, and Thay's answers. Once more I wonder if there is any way I can sneak off stage without anyone noticing. Then, towards the end, when it's apparent that time is running out and not everyone will get to ask their question, I look up.

Thay is looking directly at me. My eyes meet the soft but penetrating gaze of this Buddhist master, and suddenly my whole body is flooded with an expansive feeling of love, as if a thousand fireworks have gone off in my heart. He is still talking and answering someone else's question, but his gaze is focused directly at me, as if he can see into my very soul. I feel completely seen. I know not only that the question I couldn't put into words has been heard, but that it has somehow been answered at some deep and subtle level.

I'm sure this only lasted a minute or two, but it seems to go on forever. The image of the woman from the bible who touched the hem of Christ's garment flashes through my mind. I am that woman reaching out to touch the essence of the "Living Buddha, Living Christ." Finally, the words "you will feel light" are imprinted on my mind and felt, like thousands of stars shimmering throughout my body.

A feeling of unimaginable peace and lightness pervades my entire mind and body. I sit in absolute and utter stillness, completely unaware of the other seven hundred and ninety-nine people in the auditorium. There is only Thay and myself, in this mystical moment beyond time and space. I don't want to move a single muscle. I could stay here forever. I'm aware of Thay closing off the morning session. I feel the sound of the meditation bell ripple through my body in a delightful circular motion. As the sound dissolves back into the silence it arose from, I feel like I too might dissolve back into that same silence.

In a dreamlike state, I slowly find my way off stage and walk back to my dorm room. I feel like I am literally floating, although I am infinitely aware of every step I take. It seems as if I am seeing with new eyes. Everything seems softer, a bit out of focus. I actually feel like I'm a bit high, although I haven't smoked a joint since my rebellious teens. I'm sure I have some kind of perma-grin on my face and stars in my eyes.

I Am Solid, I Am Free

I skip lunch today. I feel absolutely no desire or need for physical food. I have been nourished by a kind of food that feeds the deepest part of my soul. My heart has been awakened and is in a wide-open, vulnerable state. Even the outer covering of my skin seems transparent, like I can somehow breathe through every tiny pore. I know that all I need right now is to let this experience slowly sink into my body and psyche.

I walk reverently through the UBC Rose Garden. The fragrance of the roses and the experience I've had with Thay seem to intermingle. I feel the deep red beauty of the roses in my soul. It's not a thought about the roses, but rather an experience of feeling and sensing the roses with all of my senses fully alive. I feel like the roses love me, and I love them in return.

I find myself slowly wandering back to the dormitory for the usual rest period, exquisitely aware of my feet on every step of the six flights up, in an effortless flow of movement and breath. As I open the door to my room, I know it looks the same as when I left it, with a few items of clothing discarded on the bed. Yet I realize that my perception of myself and my entire way of being in the world has radically shifted. It feels like a parallel universe. I'm not sure how to navigate this new world.

CHAPTER 2

The Vow of My Heart

*Everyone I saw was filled with beauty and love. There was no
distance between us. There was no hurry. There was all the time
in the world to be there and feel this love. It wasn't "my" love and
it wasn't Maharaj-ji's love. He was not different from this Presence
that surrounded everything. The whole world was filled by this
vast Presence and deep sweetness.*
Krishna Das, *Chants of a Lifetime*

I stand there, gazing dreamily out the small window of my room at
the patch of blue sky, beyond. Time seems very fluid. A thought slowly
arises, like a tiny bubble, from my consciousness. I remember that
Sister Thoai, our Dharma Family teacher, has invited us to consider
taking the Five Mindfulness Trainings,[1] Plum Village's version of
the Buddhist Precepts. This is a commitment in a formal ceremony
in front of the whole community to universal Buddhist ethics that
help one live a life in harmony with oneself, one's community, and
the world. The ceremony will take place early tomorrow morning,
on our final day of retreat. In order to receive the Five Mindfulness
Trainings, we need to write a short but formal letter of request to
Thay. Although I hadn't been sure I wanted to take them before this
morning, there is now absolutely no doubt in my mind and heart
that I want to receive these precious trainings. In our letter, we are
to answer the question "What is your deep aspiration for receiving
these trainings?" I sit down and begin to write.

Letter to Thay to Receive the Five Mindfulness
Trainings

Dear Thay,

After receiving your beautiful gaze, I feel like my heart has been awakened to a love that is beyond boundaries. Anything and everything is possible.

As I consider the Five Mindfulness Trainings this afternoon, I feel a renewed sense of passion and calling. The seeds I have watered with my practice and my prayers are ready to grow and bear fruit. I feel a deep sense of gratitude for my Christian community that has nurtured me all my life, but also a deep sense of calling to share the practice of "holy attention" that seems to have been lost from so many Christian churches. Through my yoga practice, I have been blessed with teachers from many different traditions and have come to see the rich thread of oneness in them all. It puzzles me that others cannot see this simple truth. My heart yearns for peace and to create bridges of understanding between people of different faith traditions. I believe it is the practice of holy attention, and deep listening with compassion that will make it so.

The past year has been interwoven with both sorrow and joy. My mother was diagnosed with cancer in March and passed away in early July. I was able to create space in the busyness of my life to simply be with her, to listen to her stories of both joy and suffering, to witness her pain both physical and emotional, to hold her hand, to pray with her, to breathe with her. I was able to "be with her suffering and not be overwhelmed." Somehow it felt as if all my years of practice had come together to be with my mother as she took her last breath. And now all my years of practice and seeking have come together in this moment with you, all my doubts and questions seemingly dissolved, a healing, and transformation has taken place at some level which I cannot fully fathom or understand yet.

My awakened heart is overflowing with gratitude, and I make a formal request to receive the Five Mindfulness Trainings in front of the entire community at tomorrow's ceremony.

With love and gratitude,
Vickie MacArthur

Don't Kiss and Tell

Later that afternoon, I slowly walk to the classroom where our dharma family group has been meeting all week. It still seems like I am walking in slow motion, keenly aware of the breeze caressing my skin, and that feeling of lightness in every step. Sister Thoai begins with three sounds of the bell, to help quiet our minds and still our bodies. We sit in a comfortable circle of silence and, when ready, bring our hands together in front of our heart, and bow, as a way of indicating we would like to share.

A few others share about their day and their practice, yet I am completely unaware of what they are saying. A myriad of thoughts and images has arisen from my mystical experience this morning and I can hardly contain myself. I bow in, and these thoughts and images pour out of my mouth in a mostly incoherent stream of phrases like "meeting Thay's eyes," feeling "peaceful, light, spacious," feeling like "Thay could see into my very soul." I hear myself talk about the image of the woman from the bible "touching the hem of Christ's garment," and my feeling like the "question of my heart" had been answered in silence.

As I finally look around at the people around me, I am met with confused and disbelieving looks. My mind is still not functioning in its usual way, but I am aware that I have somehow blurted out a holy, sacred experience that has not been fully processed, let alone shared. As I look up at Sister Thoai and meet her gentle gaze, I know right away that she understands, and that gives me some solace. I consider staying afterwards to talk to her, but when the final bell sounds, I slip out of the room and back to my dorm. I want to be by myself, in silence, to shed the layers of self-judgment I now feel, and to sink back into that place of complete and utter love and acceptance I had felt this morning.

Transmission of the Five Mindfulness Trainings

I am sitting in the middle of a large group of people in the very centre of the gym-cum-meditation hall. We are sandwiched between two solid lines of monastics sitting Buddha-like on either side of us. The nuns face us on one side, and monks on the other, all wearing their bright yellow sanghati robes for the formal ceremony.

The actual ceremony is something of a blur. I still have that dreamy feeling of being in love with everyone and everything. I bow and "touch the earth" many times in gratitude to all my ancestors and teachers, biological, spiritual, cultural, and to Mother Earth herself. With hands pressed together at my heart, I promise to take refuge in the Buddha, the dharma, and the sangha. With an earnest trust in my heart, I say yes to each of the Five Mindfulness Trainings as they are read aloud, not yet understanding the depth of these beautiful principles for living. After my experience yesterday with Thay, I feel like my whole life has just shifted. Like tectonic plates, this shift is causing a huge crack in the protective armoring of my carefully guarded heart.

After the ceremony is over, we are instructed to meet with our Dharma Family leader to receive our Five Mindfulness Trainings Certificate. I receive a simple embossed copy of the Five Mindfulness Trainings, dated and signed by Thich Nhat Hanh of the "42nd generation of the Lam Te (Linji) Dhyana School." I can feel the long line of ancestral teachers transmitting their love and wisdom through Thay. The certificate also reveals my new Dharma name. This name is usually bestowed by the Dharma Family Teacher; however, when Sister Thoai hands me my certificate she looks at me meaningfully and says, "Your deep aspiration to be a bridge between Buddhism and Christianity is a bit different than most aspirations, so I had to go a little higher up for your name!" My new spiritual name, "Divine Oneness of the Heart," feels like the perfect expression of my aspiration and vow to build bridges between different spiritual traditions.

Chance Encounters of the Heart

After the ceremony, we are invited for a final walking meditation
with Thay. I feel myself flowing naturally in this huge throng of
people as we slowly wend through the UBC campus, silently snaking
our way through groups of students drinking coffee and texting on
their phones. We follow the sidewalk past the clock tower, stopping
mindfully to breathe as it chimes out the hour. We stop in a grove
of trees and I remember wanting to take a picture of Thay. There
is no need now. The image of his kind and loving eyes is indelibly
imprinted in my mind and engraved on my heart.

We follow Thay back to the parking lot in front of the residences,
where a van is waiting to whisk him away. I stand completely still,
my hands joined reverently at my heart centre, as he gets into the
van, the sun reflecting off the windshield, so I cannot see his eyes.
Still, I can feel his gaze in my heart. I feel like one tiny drop in an
ocean of love.

I slowly wander back to the makeshift bookstore set up for the
retreat, a beehive of activity. Everyone wants to buy something
before leaving. Thay has written over a hundred books, on topics
ranging from anger to Zen Buddhism, and everything in between.
Hanging everywhere are beautiful calligraphies hand-painted on
parchment paper by Thay, with gathas such as "No Mud, No Lotus,"
or "Peace is every Step." If you can't afford a calligraphy, you can wear
his sayings on a T-Shirt or a sweatshirt. It seems everyone wants to
take a piece—or is it the "peace"—of Thay home with them. At one
of the tables set up near the bookstore, monks are offering DVDs of
Thay's dharma talks from this retreat. Few DVDs are left, but there
is a single one from yesterday's Questions and Answers with Thay. I
was up on stage and couldn't hear what Thay was saying, so I pick
up the DVD, slip it into my backpack, then promptly forget about it.

As I head back to my room to pack, someone from my dharma
family group asks if I'm going to go to Thay's public talk at the

Orpheum Theatre tomorrow. My heart leaps at the chance to see Thay again, but then another thought arises from somewhere deep inside. I think of Coley, Lanette's daughter.

Coley seems like an old soul in a young body, with a spiritual thirst that cannot be quenched by traditional forms and easy answers. Bedtime questions with her dad include "Why do Buddhists believe in reincarnation, but Christians don't?" As a young girl, when Coley couldn't be found playing with other kids at our church campgrounds, Lanette would often find her praying by herself in the tiny "junior chapel," tucked away close to the old growth forest. Coley has a deep love and affinity for trees and books. As I reconnect to the spacious love that Thay has awakened in my heart, I feel an urgent need to somehow get Coley close to this beloved master. Do I have hope she can be healed? Or do I simply want her to experience the miracle of love that I feel in his presence? I'm not sure. Either way, it's the same feeling that propelled me off my cushion and up onto the stage with Thay.

I make my way over to the next table, where a poster for Thay's public talk is displayed. When I inquire about tickets, I am told that they are all sold out. I mumble something about my girlfriend's daughter and cancer. Once more, the universe winks. The woman behind me taps me on the shoulder and says "I was just about to return these two tickets, but I'd like for you to have them." She refuses any money as she presses them into my hand. As I look into her eyes, I see such warmth and kindness. It almost feels like looking into Thay's eyes again.

Then, doubt. Will Coley be well enough to go? I trust in the same power that somehow got me to this retreat, the same energy that got me up on stage, close to Thay. It's the same energy that placed me at this exact moment in time, to magically receive these tickets.

Buddhists say that when the right conditions are present, things manifest. The part of me that is Christian might call these moments "God," or "grace"—not God as a grey-haired figure in the sky, pulling strings, but as the creative energy of Love that flows in and through everything and everyone. We tune into this flow of Love by simply being completely open and present. We can't be present if our mind is too full of ourselves and our own thoughts. Somehow, this retreat and encounter with Thay have slowed me down, rewired my brain, and awakened my heart to this flow of Love that is beyond my rational understanding.

CHAPTER 3

The Hermit of My Life

Back Home to Skateboards and Yoga

I arrive back home in Lethbridge to the usual chaos of a busy household. Our teenage sons and their friends play their loud staccato rap music in the front yard, while practicing skateboard tricks on their homemade skate ramp on our driveway. Emma, our black lab, races around showing her excitement at having her main walker back home. She wags her tail and runs in circles, and almost knocks me over. As I melt into Doug's welcoming arms and feel the touch of his lips, I feel the familiarity of the life we've built together over the past twenty years. At the same time, I know my life will never be the same. How will I ever be able to communicate the depth of the life-changing experience I've just had with this beloved monk? How can I possibly describe the mystical love that Thay awakened in my heart? "How are you dear?" Doug asks. His eyes search mine, as if he senses something has shifted. How will this new heart-expanding love affect our relationship and our family life?

I walk into the house we've lived in for the past ten years. Once more, everything seems achingly familiar, yet subtly different. I feel like I'm seeing everything with new eyes. My heart feels like it has no rib cage to protect it. I glance at a picture of my mother at age eighty, riding a golf cart with her sisters, a look of pure joy on her usually worried face. It's a poignant reminder that she is no longer here, but somehow I can feel her joy in this very moment, in my heart.

Later that night, in bed with Doug, I begin to share my feelings and experiences, how I felt overwhelmed at first, when all I wanted was a quiet space to grieve. I talk about my worry for Lanette and Coley. I talk about settling into the quiet rhythm of the retreat, and finally, I try to describe the mysterious force that launched me off my cushion and up onto the stage with this beloved Buddhist Master. As I describe meeting Thay's loving gaze, it feels like I am re-experiencing the timelessness of that moment. I feel the same visceral feeling in my body, expansive lightness in every cell. Doug listens quietly. I know that something is being communicated that is beyond words to express. A sacred moment with Thay becomes a sacred, intimate moment with my husband. Is there room for three in this holy love triangle? Uncertainty ripples through my heart.

I settle back into my ordinary life that doesn't seem so ordinary anymore. When I first left the silence of the retreat, all the sounds around me seemed loud and intrusive. Everyone, it seemed, was moving way too fast. I wanted to stay in the cocoon of silent wordlessness, with Thay. Everything I looked at had a soft, luminous sense of presence. I still feel that floaty feeling, as if someone has rubbed away the sharp edges of my thoughts and judgments. Could I have simply had some sort of TIA or stroke? But, no, something in me trusts that my body and soul are fine, that somehow they are integrating this sacred encounter at a much deeper level.

I continue floating effortlessly from one activity to another. Although nothing in my outer life has changed, I seem to be living life in a more relaxed state. I used to over-plan for my yoga classes, but now I seem to trust an inner voice that knows exactly what to say and where to touch, and adjust if needed. That inner lightness I'd felt with Thay seems to flow from me to others in ways I can't explain. Throughout this time, everyday activities I used to find tedious and boring take on new meaning. As a "skateboard mom" from the very first time our boys' skinny legs learned to balance on a skateboard, I'm used to spending lots of time at the skateboard park, watching Brendan and Andrew grind the rails, doing kick flips and 360s, and getting "big air" on the half pipe to the music of Mac Miller and Wiz Khalifa. Now at seventeen and thirteen, the boys refuse the pads and helmets. My heart skips a beat every time a soft body hits the hard, unyielding pavement.

I no longer have to stay and watch them all the time. Andrew, though, still needs me to get him to the park. Sometimes it's easier just to stay and read a book, even with the grinding and the rap music ricocheting like bullets through my brain. But, now, something changes at the skate park. I sit still, watching skaters of all ages as they flow in a never-ending dance of grinding and skating, and floating and landing. It's like poetry in motion against a background of wheels on concrete, voices and laughter, and the occasional F-bomb after a missed trick. It feels as if the skate park has a collective soul of its own. I feel a tender love for all the kids, as if they are my own.

It feels like I'm in a dream world. Is it all a dream? Or is this new perception of my world more real than anything I've ever known?

"If You Meet the Hermit of Your Life, Please Write to Me"

In the small backpack I had carried on retreat I find, amongst my books and journals, the DVD I purchased on the last day. I'd almost forgotten about it, but when I play *Awakening the Heart: Questions and Answers, A Deep Volition to Practice,*[2] I feel like I am back on stage. Only this time I can watch and hear Thay's answers from the audience's perspective.

I watch as the children are invited first, to ask their questions. Watching them gather around this gentle monk reminds me of the bible story of Jesus inviting children to sit on his lap while his disciples try shooing them away. "Unless you become as a little child," Jesus tells his followers, "you cannot enter the kingdom of God." There's a deep Zen message here, about going back to our beginner mind. I watch the DVD, and the little girl with the pony tail, who braves the big chair across from Thay, to ask her question.

"How did you feel when you left your country?" Next, a young Asian girl sits on the chair and asks "Where did you learn to be mindful and to breathe?" I hadn't heard Thay's answer, but now I can. With eyes full of childlike innocence and the wisdom of a lifetime, Thay tells the story of his own awakening many years ago, after climbing a mountain near his village, in Vietnam. I listen with rapt attention, as the story of his own awakening unfolds.

When Thay was nine years old, he saw a drawing of the Buddha looking so peaceful and relaxed that it inspired a deep desire in Thay to be like the Buddha. A few years later, the students from Thay's school were going up the mountain for a picnic. Thay had heard about a monk who lived up on the mountain, and was excited to try to meet him. When the students reached the top of the mountain, Thay was disappointed that the hermit was not there. While the others had a picnic, Thay stole into the woods, hoping to meet the monk. When the beautiful sound of running water led him to a well, Thay knelt down to drink the cool refreshing water. This simple act became a mystical moment of awakening for Thay.

Having drunk the water, Thay says "I had never tasted such delicious water. I felt completely satisfied. I had no more desire, including the desire to meet the monk." He then lay down and fell into such a deep sleep that, when he awoke, he did not know where he was. With regret, Thay left the well thinking, "I have tasted the most delicious water in the world."

When Thay finally joined the other boys, he did not tell them what had happened. He felt that if he talked about this mystical experience, he might lose some of the happiness. So he kept silent. In his heart, Thay believed the monk had transformed himself into a well of clear water, so he could have a private audience with him. Thay felt like he was the luckiest person on earth.

Thay ends his story by saying "I hope that everyone will have the chance to meet their hermit, their monk, maybe not in the form of a well, but maybe a tree, or a rock, or a beautiful sunset. Because you are very lucky if you have a chance to meet your hermit, your monk. Many of us may have had a chance to meet him, but did not recognize him." Looking lovingly at the children and the audience, Thay goes on to say: "So I always tell the young people, if they happen to meet their monk, their hermit, they should write to me to announce their good news. 'Dear Thay, yesterday I have met my hermit, my monk.' Maybe you will meet your monk, your hermit tomorrow, or after tomorrow. If you do, please write Thay a note and tell Thay that you have met the hermit of your life."

Once more, I am completely still like I was on stage, my awakened heart perfectly attuned to the heart of this great master. Only this time, I can hear every precious word he says. Thay's story of his awakening, I realize, foreshadows my own.

A Love Letter To Thay

August 24

Dear Thay,

I have found my hermit. I have found my monk. Only he's not really a hermit. He is very much engaged in the world, teaching and being peace. He is a deep well for a thirsty world, and I have drunk deeply.

It is with such love and gratitude that I write this letter. It has been two weeks since our retreat in Vancouver and even now that I am home, I continue to feel your presence in my heart. I'm not sure what possessed me to get up and ask a question on Friday morning, but somehow I found myself up on stage with you in front of eight hundred people! In the end however, it was not the question that mattered, only the experience of vast, unconditional love.

In that moment as I looked up and met your penetrating gaze, I felt deeply seen and deeply known, as if you could see right into my very soul. It was a holy sacred moment beyond my words to describe. I was amazed at how you continued to speak effortlessly to the other eight hundred people in the room and communicate with me at a completely different level.

In that moment of deep communion, all of my questions, all of my doubts seemed to dissolve. All that remained was a timeless feeling of deep peace, deep love, and deep joy. Although I could not physically hear your voice, every so often a word or phrase would float into my awareness like "love," or "compassion," and I would feel the energy of that quality in my heart. I heard the words "you can be with suffering and not be overwhelmed," and realized this was a gift given to me during my mother's recent illness and passing. Then there was simply a feeling of lightness and the insight of knowing who I truly am beyond the boundaries of my personality.

Coming from a Christian background, I had the image of the woman from the bible touching the hem of Christ's garment, and being healed in an instant. I was that woman reaching out to touch the Living Buddha, Living Christ. In that moment, I was changed and transformed at subtle levels that I could not even imagine and that are continuing to be revealed little by little.

Afterwards, for the rest of the day, and even now two weeks later, there is such an indescribable feeling of joy and happiness. I felt I needed to write this experience down, so I would not forget it. Often with past mystical experiences, as they have begun to fade, doubts and questions have started to surface about whether it was real. Who am I to think I could connect with a Buddhist master at this level? Why me? I confess, I have not been very mindful since it happened. My mind keeps returning to that moment, in order to anchor it deeply in my consciousness. I think about it while walking. I think about it while sitting. I think about it while eating. I awaken in the night with it. It's like the experience of falling deeply in love. Now I understand Rumi's poems of longing and union with the Beloved.

This experience is an outpouring of grace and is the answer to all my prayers, both spoken and unspoken. Lately in my practice, I seem to have reached a plateau, a dry spell. While I wouldn't call it a dark night of the soul, I call it a "blah" night of the soul. There was no joy, no juice. It felt dry and empty. And yet I kept coming back, sustained by a faith that would not let me quit, that I don't qu te understand. My prayers seemed to fall on empty ears. I have been blessed to learn and integrate many practices from many different teachers and traditions and I believe these practices have planted and nourished many good seeds. Still I have yearned and prayed for a teacher that could take me deeper.

I did not knowingly come to this retreat seeking this experience, and yet it is beyond my wildest imaginings. I came to simply "Be still and know," to be with the grief of my mother's passing. Thank you for this true gift of grace, unexpected and unsought, yet such a perfect answer to the many prayers of my heart.

With love and gratitude,
Vickie MacArthur
Divine Oneness of the Heart

After writing, I wonder how to send a letter to this world-renowned Zen Master. I check the Plum Village website and am surprised to find a "send a letter to Thay" link with an email address attached. Hand-written letters, I see, can also be sent directly to the monastery in France. How can Thay possibly read letters from thousands of students all over the world? He must get help from his monastics. With a quick prayer and a click of the keyboard, my letter is launched into cyberspace. Will Thay actually receive and read my email? Somehow, it doesn't matter. I feel as if an invisible pathway has been opened between his heart and mine, as if he already knows me better than I know myself. Then again, perhaps I've written this letter for myself. Writing has always been one way of processing my life experiences. Maybe, writing letters to Thay, even if they just stay in my journal, will help me to unpack this sacred, remarkable experience.

CHAPTER 4

Thay is Alive in Me

*Although the Guru and disciple appear to be two, it is the Guru
alone who masquerades as both. When you look in a mirror and
see your own face, you know that both are only your self.*
Swami Abhayananda Jnaneshwar

Writing to Awaken

Dear Thay,

I'm not sure how a relationship with a Zen Master works. It's not like anything I've ever experienced. It feels like something beyond time and space that is also happening right now in the flesh, in this moment and all moments. I keep pinching myself to remind me I'm still here with my feet on the ground!

I've taken you at your word and written to you to let you know "I've met the hermit of my life" in you. You are like a deep well of love that is overflowing into my life, splashing over rocks and seeping into the cracks in my heart. You are like water to my parched soul.

I think writing the letter was not only for you but also for myself, as I begin to try to understand the miracle of meeting your loving gaze. I feel like I have looked into the eyes of both the Living Buddha and the Living Christ at the same time, seeing and being seen through eyes of pure love.

Throughout my life, journaling has helped me to remember both the everyday miracles, as well as the larger stories that shape us. Writing brings clarity and understanding, connecting the dots between seemingly random events. It's a form of mindfulness that allows me to drop beneath the distractions of life, and pay attention to what's right in front of me on the page. I've started writing letters to you in my journal, as a way of keeping the sacred flame of your love alive. I know that mystical experiences like this tend to fade if not nourished, so I keep returning to that moment to imprint it more deep y in my mind and heart. I'm trusting somehow that this all-encompassing love that you have awakened in my heart will continue to reveal itsel⁻ if I simply take time to breathe and practice and to pay attention. Maybe in the future I will share these letters with you. Right now I trust thct somehow they will be received in the silence of your great heart, where time and space dissolve. For now, they will simply stay in my own journal, a testament to the unfolding of this love you have awakened in my heart.

A Pure Transmission of Love

Dear Thay,
When I first arrived at the retreat in Vancouver I felt overwhelmed by the sheer number of people bustling around. The atmosphere didn't seem conducive to the silence I needed for grieving the loss of my mother, and I nearly turned around and left. Yet something tugged at my heart to stay. Perhaps my heart already felt the calling of your heart, and what was about to unfold between us. The intimacy of gazing in your eyes was so unexpected. Like your own experience with the hermit on the mountain, revealed in a pool of clear water, I feel as if I had a private audience with you, even with hundreds of other people in the meditation hall. Still, I wonder what it would be like to sit down with you in private, to ask the true questions of my heart?

Before I sit down to write, I imagine that we are sitting together sharing a cup of tea in companionable silence. As we pour the water into the teapot, the steam rises, dissolving into the silent space between us. Although I have many questions in my heart, we don't have to say many words. The tea leaves steep in the hot water, as my questions steep in the silence of our hearts, until the words are fully infused, ready to pour themselves out onto the waiting pages of my journal.

With you, I've experienced a miracle beyond words, and the capacity of my intellect to understand. That precious moment with you continues to affect me deeply. I cannot get you out of my mind. It's as if I brought a part of you home from the retreat, with me. It's as if your presence surrounds me like my own skin.

My heart still turns somersaults when I think about you. Like the passion of a young lover, head over heels in love, I keep going back to the whole experience, to what felt like your consciousness seeking me out in the crowd, choosing me, guiding me, loving me. I can't explain the mysterious energy that catapulted me off my meditation cushion and somehow got me up on stage with you. How many conditions had to come together in that moment to manifest the meeting of our eyes and hearts and mind? Truly, I've been waiting all my life for this single encounter with a love that knows no bounds. Yet I can also see how all the other experiences of love in my life prepared me for this moment.

And you dear Thay, have you been waiting for me, for just the right moment when everything aligned perfectly for our eyes and hearts to meet? It is said that when the student is ready, the teacher appears. Does it also work the other way, so that when the teacher is ready, the student appears?

In the moment that our eyes met, it felt like you knew me completely, as if you knew all the nooks and crannies of my mind and heart. All of my past, my present, and my future came together in this one mystical moment. It was an experience of being fully seen and loved and accepted, exactly as I am, but also for who I can become. Something in me knows it is not just Thay the Buddhist master calling me. It is the timeless living Buddha, the eternal living Christ. You are simply the enlightened being showing me the Christ within myself.

After this experience, I felt so light, like I was walking on air and could float away like a cloud shifting in the sky. The five days at this retreat was supposed to be a time to go inwards, and just be with the feelings of sadness and grief after my mother's passing. However, as usual, I fell into old habit energies and found myself dealing with feelings of inadequacy, comparing myself with others, even wondering if I was grieving "properly." Yet in that transmission of unconditional love from you, all of that self-doubt was swept away.

What exactly is a transmission? Dharma Wisdom teacher Phillip Moffitt says "Transmission is most commonly described as a deep feeling of unconditional love, which is so intense it brings about inner change."[3] As I read more about transmission, I began to understand that authentic spiritual masters are able to transmit the subtle energy of their own enlightened mind to others. Somehow, this energy calls forth the disciple's own Buddha mind or Christ consciousness that transcends the person's current level of awareness. Spiritual transmission seems to expand our capacity for growth on whatever spiritual path we walk.

I don't really need to rely on the words of others, for I have received a direct experience in my heart. In that moment of transmission with you, I felt a deep merging, a deep love and compassion, an intimate connection that cannot be put into words. I was aware that you were still speaking to the audience, yet on another level you were communicating directly with me. I was changed in the wink of an eye, deeply merging with both you and the Source of all. I finally understood St. Teresa of Avila and her mystical marriage with the Beloved. Even now, I long for this holy passion.

Still I wonder, why me? What did you see in me? What was it in me that was open to you? Perhaps these deep questions have no answer, except in silence. Yet, I am filled with wonder and gratitude. I was in a vulnerable space of grieving, confused and full of doubt. Now I have received this divine outpouring of water that is soaking the parched land of my soul.

You have awakened my heart. I feel myself coming alive again, ready to live deeply in every moment, to fully inhabit my new dharma name, Divine Oneness of the Heart. When Sister Thoai handed me my Five Mindfulness Trainings certificate, and said that, since my aspiration was different, she had to request a name from "higher up," I wondered what she meant. Was it you, dear Thay, who bestowed this name because you could see into my "inter-spiritual" heart, a heart that wants to be a bridge for peace between different religions and traditions? Could you see the love and deep yearning I have for God, for Buddha, for Christ, for Allah, for Krishna, for the Ultimate Love that is known by so many names, and by no name at all? It will, I know, take a lifetime to grow into this dharma name.

Something has shifted in me. Something has been planted, like a seed ready to sprout and grow out of the darkness. Somehow, all my life experience as a mother, a lover and wife, a minister, and a yoga teacher have provided the rich fertile soil for this unfolding. I feel a deep calling to share the gift and passion I have for yoga and Eastern-based meditation practices with the Christian community that has nurtured me all my life. I have a strong feeling that my dharma, my soul's purpose, is to integrate these practices of mindfulness and "holy attention" into my Christian heritage, to be a bridge of understanding and light between faiths. I feel as if you have blessed me, empowered me to teach through this direct transmission of love.

I have been born anew. Jesus said that new wine cannot be put into old wine skins. It's time to shed my old skin and habit energy of doubt and judgment, comparisons, feeling small, and step into this new way of being, this new energy you have transmitted to me. I know this experience will continue to reveal itself in new ways in my life. I now have a teacher who is not limited by time or by space. That teacher is you, in me. I just need to recognize my new self.

Buddha is Breathing, Christ is Sitting

Dear Thay,
Last night I watched an online video of your dharma talk from Estes Park, Colorado. I lit a candle and sat quietly on my cushion in the sanctuary of my meditation room, with the soft glow of the computer screen's dim light. A few clicks of my keyboard, and there you were. It was so good to see your face, and hear your voice again, yet there

was something more. It felt like our physical encounter had somehow created a heart connection that goes well beyond the usual online screen presence. I've listened to online talks by other teachers, but as you spoke, there was something familiar and intimate, as if once more something was being transmitted beyond the words you said. Even across the miles, I could feel that enlivening of my heart centre as you invited three sounds of the large bell, calling me home to my body and my breath, and the vitality of this moment. Then the comforting sound of your voice repeating the gathas:[4]

> I invite the Buddha (Christ) to breathe with me.
> I invite the Buddha (Christ) to sit with me.
> I don't have to breathe, I don't have to sit.

I sat perfectly still and invited both the Buddha and the Christ, and you, dear Thay, to breathe and sit with me. I smiled as I imagined all of us sitting on one cushion together. What a relief to finally let go of control. I let go of trying so hard to meditate and quiet my mind. Instead, I simply invited these great spiritual beings to be present in me. I could literally feel my face soften, and the tension in my shoulders release.

> The Buddha (Christ) is breathing, the Buddha (Christ) is sitting.
> I enjoy the breathing, I enjoy the sitting.

Yes, I can trust the Buddha in me. I can trust the Christ in me. I can enjoy this practice, feeling the space on the in-breath, and the release on the out-breath. I feel the weight of my body sitting in the chair. I feel my mind naturally becoming quieter. It feels so healing.

> Buddha (Christ) is the breathing, Buddha (Christ) is the sitting.
> I am the breathing, I am the sitting.

My mind concentrated, I can feel the subtle shift in both words and energy as my breath slows down and becomes softer and smoother. I can begin to recognize the quality of the Buddha and the Christ in my very breath. I can feel their compassion transmitted over two thousand years and more. I can feel the timelessness of your love transmitted only weeks ago. Perhaps I can become a bit less attached to the "me" I think I am.

> *There is only the breathing, there is only the sitting.*
> *There is no one breathing, there is no one sitting.*

I start to feel lightness in my body and mind, similar to what I felt when I looked into your eyes. Every cell of my body tingles. I simply relax into it then find myself wondering if "I" will disappear. I laugh. I'm not a Buddha yet! I've only just begun to explore who this "I" is.

> *Peace while breathing. Peace while sitting.*
> *Peace is the breathing, Peace is the sitting.*

I feel a deep sense of peace and contentment. There's absolutely nothing I need in this moment, other than to bask in your love. My heart is full of gratitude. I've read that sometimes masters will give their students mantras or koans to practice with. I feel like this is mine, and that its meaning will continue to unfold as I practice embodying the qualities of the Buddha, the Christ, and you, dear Thay. I seem to have touched a deep well of peace within. I've got a long ways to go to "no-self" or emptiness, but somehow you've given me a small glimpse of "inter-being" just by looking in your eyes.

Pregnant with the Buddha

In Zen Buddhism, the teacher may propose a koan, and if teacher and student are lucky and skillful enough, the student's mind of enlightenment will be touched... She entrusts the koan to her store consciousness, just as a woman who is pregnant trusts her body to nourish her baby.

Thich Nhat Hanh, *Cultivating the Mind of Love*

September 3

Dear Thay,

It seems strange to write to a Buddhist monk about this, but for some reason I feel like I can tell you the deepest secrets of my heart. Since coming home from the retreat, I've had this feeling of fullness and ripeness, like a tiny seed has been planted deep within me. It reminds me of how I felt when I was pregnant with my sons. I loved being pregnant. I didn't have many side effects that other women seem to have. I felt full of life, so radiant and alive. So it seems strange to be having these visceral sensations of new life in my body. Here I am, a menopausal woman, feeling that familiar sense of fullness in my breasts and softness in my belly. Like a woman ripe with child, I find myself spontaneously bringing my hands to my belly, feeling the aliveness of my breath beneath my palms. I wonder if there's any possible way I could actually be pregnant? Not! At my age, that would truly be a miracle, but then seeing myself reflected in your eyes of love has been a miracle in itself.

This experience has also touched sensual feelings of love and longing in me that aren't sexual so much as they connect to the universal longing of all creation for union and wholeness. How can one moment, looking into the eyes of an eighty-five-year-old celibate Buddhist monk, awaken these feelings in me? It seems like a great cosmic joke. I've been having wild dreams about being pregnant and having a new baby, and I believe that dreams are how the unconscious part of ourself tries to get our attention, to reveal a forgotten part of us. Just as you have taught, I will not ignore these dreams and feelings, but will bring them out into the light of my practice, and see where they lead.

In your captivating book, *Cultivating the Mind of Love,* you say that the seed of mindfulness can be described as the womb of the Buddha, that we are all pregnant with the Buddha. Perhaps the mind of love is the seed that you have touched alive in me. As you say, "Awakening to our mind of love is the moment the practice begins."[5] That baby Buddha has been waiting patiently to be born, and I have to give him a chance. In that one moment with you, I was filled with bodhicitta, the mind of enlightenment, the mind of love. Now it is up to me to nourish it and allow it to grow, just like a baby in the womb of my heart.

Perhaps the Christ is also waiting to be born in me. I am reminded of the angel Gabriel's visit to Mary, so innocent, so pure, so willing, yet also filled with doubt and fear as to what giving birth to Love incarnate would mean. There were no witnesses when Gabriel came, and Mary pondered these things in secret, in her heart.

Although the meditation hall was filled with people, the gaze of love that passed between us was both offered and received in the silence of my waiting heart. Like Mary, I too have kept this mystical meeting a secret in that same heart. I have shared a small part of that meeting with my husband and a few close friends. Yet words cannot express the true depth and intimacy of that moment. How can anyone hope to understand what only true lovers share in secret?

Like Mary, I know many will not understand. How long can I carry and nourish this secret love before it either dies, or I give birth to whatever form this seed of love grows into? It is a lonely and difficult path to walk. There's no one I can talk to, and already, part of me is filled with doubt. A part of me knows that this gift of love has been indelibly imprinted on my heart and can never be forgotten. It is beyond my understanding. Yet there is also the rational part of my mind that is full of doubt and asks how this happens and how can it be true? Is it just my imagination? Who am I to think that a Zen Master somehow saw me in a crowd of people, and watered the seed of love and enlightenment in me? Then again, who was Mary but a young peasant, willing to give birth to love incarnate? It may be a small thing compared to Mary's child, but the gift of love can never be measured.

And so I will wait and watch, patiently nourishing these twin babies, the Buddha and Christ, growing in me. I will breathe and walk mindfully through rocky paths of my own judgment, rejection, fear and doubt. I will keep the "holy flame" of love alive in a world that so desperately needs light. I will water the lotus growing out of the mud.

PART 2

Kindling the Flame

The path of love is a fire within the heart that burns away the
veils of separation, emptying us of ourself so that we can come to
experience our innermost state of union.
Llewellyn Vaughan-Lee, *Love is a Fire*

CHAPTER 5

Who Is Thay? Who Am I?

A "Rock-Star" Buddhist Teacher

Dear Reader:

Like anyone who has just fallen in love, I wanted to learn all I could about Thich Nhat Hanh. Before I left for the retreat in Vancouver, I didn't know much about this simple Buddhist monk who is loved by millions of people worldwide. I had read his *Living Buddha, Living Christ* the year before, and while his words had touched me, they hadn't sparked the unquenchable fire I now feel in my heart. Now, I wanted to know everything about this beloved teacher who, in one timeless moment, opened my eyes to a love beyond anything I have ever felt or imagined.

I've begun to read and watch everything I can about him only to realize that this is no ordinary Buddhist teacher. Thay has led an extraordinary life of love and compassion and sacrifice. Thich Nhat Hanh (Thay) is one of the best-known and most respected Buddhist masters in the world today. This global spiritual leader, poet, artist, and peace activist is loved and respected for his simple, yet in-depth teachings and bestselling writings on mindfulness and peace. As a writer, Thay has published well over one hundred titles in English, and sold millions of books in North America alone. Instrumental in bringing Buddhism to the West, Thay has founded many monasteries, and has built a dedicated worldwide monastic community, as well as thousands of sanghas, and local practice groups.

Born in central Vietnam in 1926, Thay entered Tu Hieu Temple in Hue City, at the age of sixteen. As a young monk in the early 1950's, Thay was actively engaged in the movement to renew Vietnamese Buddhism. During the Vietnam War, the monastery was confronted with the issue of whether to adhere to the contemplative life, or help those around them who were suffering the tumult of war. Thay chose to do both, and in doing so founded the Engaged Buddhism movement. His life has since been dedicated to the work of inner transformation through mindfulness, for the benefit of individuals and society.

In 1961 Thay travelled to the United States to study Comparative Religion at Princeton University and the following year went on to teach and research Buddhism at Columbia University. He returned to Vietnam in 1963 to play a leading role there in the Buddhist movement for peace and social action. In 1966, shortly after receiving the lamp transmission from his teacher to teach, Thay travelled back to the US to make the case for peace and to call for an end to hostilities in Vietnam. There he met Dr. Martin Luther King Jr., who nominated him for the Nobel Peace Prize in 1967, calling him an "Apostle of Peace." As a result of his time in America, both North and South Vietnam denied him the right to return to Vietnam. So began Thay's long exile of 39 years.

Thich Nhat Hanh continued to travel widely, spreading the message of peace and reconciliation, and advocating for an end to the Vietnam War. He also continued to teach, lecture and write on the art of mindfulness and peace. In 1982 Thay established his first monastery, Plum Village, in southwestern France. Under Thay's spiritual leadership, Plum Village has grown into a thriving spiritual practice centre, with over two hundred resident monastics, and over 10,000 visitors every year from all over the world. Thich Nhat Hanh's teachings have continued to spread, with monasteries opening across the globe. Thay's love for children and young people has inspired Wake-Up, a worldwide movement that is teaching a whole new generation of young people how to incorporate mindfulness into their everyday lives, as well as training teachers to teach mindfulness in schools. Thich Nhat Hanh has had a profound impact all across the world, with the practices of mindfulness being incorporated at every level of society, from grade schools to universities, through corporations like Google, through healthcare training at Harvard Medical School, and through the many retreatants who bring his philosophy and practices back to their own communities.

Thay Beyond Words

Teaching is not done by talking alone. It is done by how you live
your life. My life is my teaching. My life is my message.
Thich Nhat Hanh, *At Home in the World*

September 12

Dear Thay,

Before I left for the retreat in Vancouver, I had no idea who you were let alone the extent of your teachings and reputation. I had read a few of your articles in the *Shambhala Sun* about mindfulness and walking meditation and I had loved, in *Living Buddha, Living Christ,* how beautifully you connected the teachings of both. At the retreat, your practices first struck me as deceptively simple. Now I see that they were beyond the understanding of my rational mind. Day by day, as I sat in the crowded gymnasium-cum-meditation hall, I felt a bit lonely and lost. The yoga and meditation retreats I'd attended before were much smaller and intimate. In Vancouver, you seemed so remote, on the far side of the ocean of people that filled the meditation hall. Then I looked into your eyes, and everything changed in that instant. Now there is a sense of familiarity, as if an invisible thread has woven our hearts together.

Since returning home, so many questions have flooded my mind. There is so much I want to know about you. Who is this Buddhist monk who has completely captured my heart? What stories and events have shaped your life? How did you learn to transmit the powerful loving energy that awakened my heart? So many questions! I can't sit at your feet in the traditional guru/disciple relationship, but you have left a paper trail of books and writing and practices, and online dharma talks to listen to. That seems like a good place to start, only where do I start? You have written dozens upon dozens of books on everything from anger to Zen practice. I want to read them all, but I find myself drawn more to your own personal stories and journals than the actual teachings and philosophies of Buddhism.

Your journals as a young monk in *Fragrant Palm Leaves* have such a tender, innocent quality, as you discover the many cultural differences between living in the United States compared to the quiet simplicity of your home in Vietnam. I can almost feel the longing of your heart for the wild, rugged beauty of Phuong Buoy. I can feel your sadness and grief for your country and friends and students as Vietnam spirals into war and chaos.

In *Cultivating the Mind of Love* you tell the story of falling in love with a beautiful nun. As I read, I can feel the excitement in the young monk's heart, as he gazed at this pure and beautiful young nun. I can feel the anguish and confusion in your heart as you felt the conflicting energies between the powerful human urge to give in to this sensual all-consuming love, and the deep aspiration in your heart to serve humanity and live out this love as a Buddhist monk. I find myself wondering about the connection between them both. Perhaps they "inter-are."

Somehow your private thoughts and feelings touch my heart as if we are once more sharing that mystical moment in Vancouver. Every time you said a word like "peace" or "lightness," I could feel the energetic quality of that word in my heart. It's a similar experience now, just reading your words on the page. I don't know how to explain it other than to say that I can almost "feel" your experience in my body. It's different from reading stories by other teachers and authors. It's not exactly a physical sensation, but rather the subtle vibration of my heart held within your great heart of love. It's as if you are teaching me from a much deeper place of knowing than mere words or books. Is this the felt experience of "inter-being" beyond the words themselves?

God, Guru, and Self are One

Invoking the energy of an enlightened being can set your practice
on fire, bring sweetness to a dry meditation, and open you to the
subtle, protective and transforming forces of the cosmos.
Sally Kempton, *Meditation for the Love of It*

October 3

Dear Thay,

On the way home from the Vancouver retreat, I picked up a book by Sally Kempton called *Meditation for the Love of It.* That seems to be one of many gifts you have graced me with—a deeper love for meditation, a deeper longing in my soul for God, the desire for that holy communion that can't be put into words. You teach that all of us already have the seed of awakening within us. You simply touched that seed like the rays of the sun, helping it to sprout and grow.

As I contemplate my experience of inner awakening with you at the retreat, and read Sally's book, I find that her words help give voice to my experience and practice of meditation. Sally talks about both the intimate and universal nature of the guru/disciple relationship. Having "woken up" herself in the presence of an Indian master who worshiped reality as divine energy (or Shakti), she has been able to help me explore and understand the subtle energetic quality of this relationship I seem to be having with you.

I am puzzled and delighted by the depth of feeling you have awakened in my heart. I am consumed by a newfound love both for meditation and for the simple, intimate pleasure of watching my own breath rising and falling. I've always been blessed by the discipline of a regular yoga and meditation practice. However, now when I wake up in the morning, I can't wait to get to my meditation cushion, and simply breathe and bask in the feelings of love and peace that wash over me. Sometimes, later in the day, as I pass the door to my meditation room, I glance at your picture on my altar, and it seems like you're trying to catch my eye again. I find myself spontaneously drawn to drop everything just so I can sit and breathe with you.

No matter when I practice, I light the candle in front of your picture as a way of invoking your presence. Somehow I am instantly transported back to that moment our eyes met. It is a touchstone, a magnet from your heart to mine. Sally says that invoking the guru is never about worshipping an actual human being, so although I have a deep sense of devotion for you as my teacher, something in me also knows that you are simply the form through which God or Divine Love is revealing the universal pattern of love and "inter-being," as you call it. It is like your body and heart forms the container for that power, and it is somehow merging with mine.

Sally Kempton writes "It is one of the great mysteries in this universe: how the universal power of grace, the principle of divine help, roots itself in the person of an enlightened teacher, then flows into anyone who connects with that teacher."[6] Somehow, my connecting with you has also linked me to your teacher, and to all the sacred lineage of teachers in the Lam Te (Linji) Dhyana School, perhaps all the way back to the Buddha himself. I can feel and touch their ancestral presence through you. At the same time, it's as if you have initiated me into a love affair that is beyond the boundaries of any one religion. I am standing in the swell of an underground river that flows deep in the heart of the cosmos. With the opening of my inner world comes this new-found energy, and power to practice.

What exactly is a guru? The term has been given a bad rap here in North America and often with good reason. Sadly, some self-described "gurus" have tainted the title, seduced by the power of money and sex and fame. Many vulnerable students have entrusted their heart to a guru, only to become victims of verbal, sexual and other kinds of abuse. No wonder most people are suspicious of anyone who calls themself a guru. Perhaps that's the point. Someone who calls themself a guru is often not one at all. Fully enlightened teachers like you are often the most humble and loving beings, slowly revealing the layers of their true "enlightened self" to each one, according to our receptivity and readiness.

Many yoga students from India and other places lovingly call their teachers "guruji." The endearing name we call you is Thay. It's a name that, whenever I repeat or say it, creates a tender feeling in my heart. I've read somewhere that "Thay" simply means "teacher" in Vietnamese, but I wonder if it denotes a deeper kind of spiritual teacher. There are so many different levels of teachers. The guru is sometimes defined as one who guides us from darkness to light, yet in India the word is often used for all teachers worthy of respect. Here in the West, we have many wise and generous spiritual teachers, although, with the rise in popularity of yoga and meditation, we also have teachers who seem to be using spiritual teachings as a way of amassing money and fame.

Satguru: A Teacher of Truth

The Buddha is not a person outside of us, but the energy
of mindfulness, concentration and insight in us. We have the seeds
of compassion in us.
Thich Nhat Hanh, *Awakening of the Heart*

Dear Thay,
It is said that when the student is ready, the teacher appears. I believe we all have an inner teacher who guides us if we listen to the gentle nudges of our heart. In Christianity we might call that the guidance of the Holy Spirit. In Buddhism, you might call it the energy of mindfulness. Over the years, I've learned to trust my intuition and knowing. Somehow, in one timeless moment, the universe lined up and that inner teacher brought me to you. So many conditions came together at the right time: a chance comment by my friend about your retreat in Vancouver, a willingness to register for the retreat without knowing much about you, my mother's illness and passing, my determination to stay at the retreat despite my

doubt and grief, and finally the mysterious force that pushed me up on stage, not so I could ask a question, but so I could look into your eyes and be transformed in the naked truth of that moment. It truly is a miracle of mindfulness and inter-being for that moment to unfold so perfectly.

I have been practicing and studying yoga and meditation now for almost eighteen years, and I have been blessed and inspired by many wise and kind teachers. I have done my best to practice diligently. All of these teachers have shared the fruits of their practices, giving me a firm grounding for a yoga practice that embodies awareness of the subtleties of breath and feelings, and thoughts observed with compassion and loving kindness. I am so grateful to each and every one of these teachers and for the practices they have instilled in me, but it's very clear that none of them were my master, what in Sanskrit is called "satguru." While all of these teachers were enlightened to varying degrees and shared their love and compassion, none of them had the ability to transmit the kind of love and energy that I felt with you. In India, this kind of teacher, a "satguru," has the ability to impart a "taste" of enlightenment to others until they can fully realize it for themselves. Such a master has the capacity to awaken you to the vast love you already are. That love can never be fully expressed through words. It can only be felt in the depth of our hearts.

So I am slowly starting to realize the immense gift of what I have received from you. It is a subtle transmission of your fully awakened state of love. Yet it's not exactly "you" as a separate self or teacher, and it's not exactly "me" as a separate self or student. It's more like the power of your loving gaze watered the seed of enlightenment in me that had already been watered by my practice and by all the many moments of love in my life. And it's not only something in memory. It's a constant stream of love from your heart to mine, from all the Buddhas and all the Christs throughout time and space, and from the very heart of God to and through all creation.

So, dear Thay, when I invite you to be present in my meditation and in my daily life, I am opening myself up to your inner state of clarity and love. It's like an inner state of aliveness opens in me, where I can search out the dark and dim places in my still-sleeping self, and allow my own light to shine a bit brighter along the way. Of course, I'm not a Buddha yet. I'm not a Christ yet. I'm not enlightened yet, but I have received tiny precious kernels of insight on the path. You teach that enlightenment is the path itself, and I seem to be on the path of true love and devotion, or bhakti, as it's known in yoga. I can feel myself opening to the love that you live and embody and that has been embodied by all the great beings throughout time and space. I'm beginning to feel that the love of both the Buddha and the Christ are woven together, in me.

Happy Birth (Continuation) Day Thay

Breathing in, I know my sangha is still there, around me,
breathing with me.
Breathing out, I smile to my sangha.
My sangha is not exactly outside of me.
Actually it's inside of me and I can bring it home.
Thich Nhat Hanh, *Dharma Talk, October, 2011*

October 11
Dear Thay,
My thoughts turn to you today, on this your 85th Birthday. With the Buddhist teachings of "no birth, no death," at Plum Village you say "Happy Continuation Day" instead of "Happy Birthday." Words have powerful effects on our thoughts and consciousness. We are a continuation of all our ancestors, both biological and spiritual, and all who have gone before us in one continuous stream. So Happy Continuation Day, my beloved teacher. I am your continuation with each sweet breath I breathe, and each careful step I take on our precious planet. Thank you for awakening my heart to the vast ocean of love that you are. May you continue to awaken hearts wherever you go.

In some ways I feel a kind of sadness to have met you so late in your life, and yet my heart trusts that we have met at exactly the right time. I am already planning to visit Plum Village next year. Perhaps I will come for the 21-Day Retreat in June. I wonder, what will it be like to be in your presence again? Will I have a chance to look in your eyes once more? Although you are still full of so much energy and vitality, I wonder how long you will continue to keep up your full schedule of traveling and teaching. It must be very hard on your physical body. What love you must have in your heart to continue to share these precious teachings, along with your monastic community. You are a true Buddha, sharing the mind of love with all who are ready, and not giving up until all are carried safely to the other shore.

Sangha, a loving community, is the net that can help carry us all to the other shore of love. In your last dharma talk at the retreat, you talked about how important a sangha, or community of practice, is. I could feel the powerful effects of hundreds of us practicing together in Vancouver in my own mind and body. "It's very difficult to sustain the practice by yourself" you said. "When you get home, either join a sangha, or start your own."

I've taken you at your word, dear Thay, and started a sangha here where I live. Since Lethbridge is a smaller city, there were no Plum Village sanghas, and not really any meditation groups either. Starting a sangha seems to be a natural expansion of my practice of yoga, and my yoga community. In fact, some of my students had already been asking me if I taught meditation. I smiled when they asked this, because what else is yoga but a meditation on the body and the breath, both in movement and stillness?

Still, I feel a bit nervous about beginning the practice of sangha-building by myself. It feels so lonely. Yet I trust the seed of love that you planted in my heart is meant to be shared, and it feels like the transmission of your love has somehow empowered and blessed me to take this next step. Sangha is both the practice and the fruit of the practice. I can trust in the deep longing in my own heart for friends and community on the path.

So my gift to you, dear Thay, is our early morning sangha here in Lethbridge. Of course the best kind of gift is one where there is no giver or receiver, just a flow of unconditional love. We call ourselves Dawning Light Sangha, for truly the light of your love is just peeking over the horizon and shining into our hearts. We meet on Tuesday mornings at 6:30 a.m., before most people have to work. So it was very fitting that we met on this, your "continuation day." Of course you were there as usual in our sitting, in our walking, and in the sound of the bell. We meet at the Community of Christ Church here in Lethbridge, where I also serve as a minister. My family has been a part of this denomination for many generations. I can feel the immense love that has trickled down to me through this Christian community of faith.

"If you build it, they will come," the saying goes. We have been meeting for almost a month now. To begin with, I simply put the invitation out on my website and social media. I was amazed at how people who have already been touched in some way by your teachings, through your books and online talks, then showed up. It's as if the magnet of your presence in my heart is attracting them, like butterflies are drawn to flowers. There has been a deep longing for support and sharing practices in this community, I think, and it is manifesting through you and me, and this one small sangha in this corner of the world.

CHAPTER 6

Slowing Down to Love More Deeply

Maternal love is our first taste of love, the origin of all feelings of love. Our mother is the teacher who first teaches us love...Without my mother I could never have known how to love.
Thich Nhat Hanh, *A Rose for Your Pocket*

My Mother's Parting Gift

October 24

Dear Thay,

It seemed as if, when you looked into my eyes, you saw all of me—my past, my future, my hopes, fears, doubts and dreams, and my tender heart grieving the loss of my dear mother. After learning that her cancer was terminal, I made a conscious decision to let everything else go, in preparation for letting her go. I knew it was important to slow down and simply be with my mother during these precious final months of her life. I had the feeling that everything in my life had come together in this moment, and that both my mother and I needed to take this journey together. Cancer and other debilitating diseases have a way of reminding us of what's important.

With prayers and determination, the way opened fairly quickly for my mother to move from Calgary where she lived, down to palliative care in Lethbridge to be close to me and my family. I know the move was difficult for her, but she comes from a family of strong faith and strong women. Although her cancer was progressing rapidly, and her short-term memory was deteriorating, we shared a lot of precious moments. We had a few walks around the lake next to the nursing home where she lived, but she tired easily. More often, we would sit in a small sunroom overlooking the lake, watching life pass by in the form of walkers and joggers and mothers pushing strollers, as the lake reflected the sky above. These were simple moments of just being, and true gifts to me in the busyness of my life.

My mother shared many stories from her life; some I'd heard before, some were new. They were like tiny snapshots of her life. Some happy, some sad, some accepting, some tinged with regret. My mother knew she was dying and perhaps knew at a deeper level that she had less time than we thought. These stories were her way of reviewing her life. And so I sat with her, and listened...and laughed...and cried...as a daughter and as a witness to both her joy and her sorrow.

My mother's growing dementia meant she often told the same story over and over again, as if her brain were caught in a groove it couldn't get out of. One of the stories she told was the story of my birth, and how much she wanted a girl, what with two boys already! After a short, intense labour, the doctor said "Mrs. Richards, you have a beautiful baby girl!" With newfound energy after the hard work of labor, my mother raised herself up off the bed and said with a smile "Really, I finally have a baby girl?"

From the birthing bed to her dying bed, I can still hear the soft raspy sound of my mother's voice and see her feebly raise herself off the bed as she told me the story of my birth over and over and over again. I can still see the look of love in her pain-filled eyes. Yes, I've known what it's like to be "seen" with the eyes of love, yet sometimes I forget.

Finally, as the cancer began to take her, I sat with her, breathed with her, sang with her, cried with her, prayed with her, and finally when it was time, watched her take her last precious breath. It seemed like all my years of practice and the faith that she had handed down to me had come together so I could be there for her. Along with her faith, my mother's parting gift was the reminder simply to slow down and to savour each precious moment with the ones we love. I made a silent vow in my heart not to let my life speed up again, but to take time to cultivate a sense of living life from a gentle unfolding, instead of a "to do" list with checkmarks.

One month later, I looked into your eyes, dear Thay, and received that same gaze of unconditional love. It was l ke being seen through my mother's eyes once more. It was the eyes of Divine Love that sees us all, if we simply slow down, and allow ourselves to be truly seen.

My Whirlpool of Busyness

We have created a society in which the rich get richer and the poor get poorer, and in which we are so busy and caught up in our own immediate problems that we cannot afford to be aware of what is going on with the rest of the human family and planet Earth.
Thich Nhat Hanh, *The World We Have*

Dear Thay,

Before my mother fell sick with car cer, my life was filled to the brim with meetings, events, classes, and more. Even my church and spiritual life was becoming just one more thing to do I found myself giving out of a cup that was half full instead of a cup that was overflowing. Like everyone else, I was also plugged into my technology twenty-four seven, on my iPhone, my iPod, and my iPad, until my "I" finally quit. My life was a continuous blur of one activity after another. I would fall into bed exhausted, then toss and turn all night as my mind tried to shut out the barrage of thoughts and images. Even with my regular yoga practice, I began to wonder why my body felt so tense and tight, and why that pain in my back just wouldn't go away.

There never seemed enough time for a walk in the park, or a cozy cup of tea with a friend. Something else always needed attention. I felt tired and cranky most of the time. I'd snap at my kids and husband for no reason. I was that hamster running cn a wheel, unable to get off.

Yes, I had a dedicated yoga and meditation practice. I knew how to move and breathe, and sit and "be still." Yet the calm seemed to disappear as the whirlwind of my activities swept me through my day. Something in me knew that there's another way, a gentler way, a kinder way of being with myself and with others. Yet I wasn't sure how to get there, how to unplug and unhook from my busy frenetic over-scheduled life.

A Living Breathing Practice

Dear Thay,
Somehow, your practices of mindful breathing, walking, eating, and simply savouring each moment are helping to slow me down in ways that I never thought possible. These simple practices seem to be helping me to keep the silent promise I made to my mother on her death bed, of taking time to truly live and savour everything in my life exactly as it is, instead of rushing headlong into the future.

Since coming home from the retreat in Vancouver, my way of inhabiting the world has changed. My brain seems to have been re-wired in a way that allows me to drop my worries and let go of my long to-do list. Some of those activities don't seem so urgent anymore. My commitment to the Fifth Mindfulness Training means I have given up the glass of wine I used to enjoy on weekends to relax. I've realized that in a society where young people binge drink for "fun" until they pass out, and so many families are ravaged by the effects of alcoholism, I want to set a better example for my two young sons.

I also feel more connected to nature, and can almost feel the trees breathing around me as I walk through the forest with Emma, my black lab, scampering ahead. I now prefer solitude, rather than a never-ending schedule of social events where people are more interested in talking about the latest scandal or social media sensation than connecting with depth. I think I'm becoming a bit of a hermit. I find myself reading books on spirituality, as well as watching online talks with spiritual themes of love. I read your books and other writings and seem to understand them with a wisdom that feels like a kind of knowing, deep in my soul.

I've read poems by Sufi poets Rumi and Hafiz before, but now I have a direct experience of being "intoxicated" with divine love (who needs wine anymore!) I read books from different traditions about the relationship between guru and disciple, and am reassured that I'm not completely crazy (well, maybe I am, but I'm in good company.) Others have also felt—and feel!—this mystical love for great spiritual beings like Buddha and Christ, or for the many teachers and saints who have embodied this divine love through the years.

I have been changed in the "twinkling of your eyes" in both dramatic and subtle ways that I am still discovering. I continue to begin my day with the practice of yoga and meditation, however, those practices are shifting and growing in me, as I stretch and grow beyond the skin of my old practice. As a morning person, I have always started my practice by moving and breathing and stretching to awaken, feeling the stiffness in my joints beginning to release, and enjoying the feeling of my body expressing itself through different postures. However, now I feel a sense of effortlessness as body and breath are synchronized, awake to the prana and energy of life that infuses all living things. I always take a few moments to rest in "savasana" (corpse pose,) and allow myself to surrender deeply back to the earth. My physical hatha yoga practice helps prepare both my body and my mind so I can sit comfortably still in meditation practice.

The altar I've set up in my meditation room is filled with sacred pictures and objects I've collected over the years. Now I have a picture of you sitting between a statue of the Buddha and a picture of Christ. I begin my practice by lighting a candle and some incense. I watch as the incense slowly wafts upwards, disappearing into the air, or drifting through my open window towards the sky above. Somehow I believe it reaches you, and the Buddha and Christ, beyond time and space. I then take a few moments to breathe and centre on my cushion, then invite three sounds of the bell. With the first sound, I invite the living Buddha to breathe and sit with me. With the second sound, I invite the living Christ to breathe and sit with me. Finally, with the third sound of the bell, I invite you, dear Thay, to breathe and to sit with me. I know that Buddha, Christ, and you and I are all connected. We "inter-are."

We all settle into this shared breath together. I feel my breath begin to slow down and deepen, as a sense of calm and ease envelops mind and body. Thoughts and feelings arise that seem to distract me, but I remember to let them go, until the bell on my meditation timer signals the end of my practice.

In the past, my sense of calm and ease would disappear. Now, I find that the Buddha and the Christ, and you, get up off the cushion with me, and follow me into the kitchen where I mindfully prepare my coffee. I'm still in touch with my breath, feeling my feet on the ground. I hear the sound of the kettle boiling, and watch as the steam arises, like the incense. I enjoy the smell of the coffee brewing, then savour the first taste. As I prepare for the rest of my day, I am in touch with the embodied sense of aliveness that infused my morning practice. Later in the day I try to practice "dog walking meditation" with Emma. I love to watch her as she takes time to explore every scent along the path, and as I feel each step along the way.

Yes, of course, my mindfulness fades in and out through the day as my mind is distracted with a multitude of tasks, but now a thin thread of awareness is also woven into my day. It's the thread of my own breath that links me to the energy of mindfulness, and the continued presence of love embodied in the Buddha, the Christ and you. This is truly the miracle of mindfulness. I imagine my mother smiling as she quietly sips her tea out of a delicate shamrock teacup somewhere beyond.

CHAPTER 7

Seeing With the Eyes of Love

The nature poem reminds me of when I was younger and used to dance and just celebrate being alive outside at night in my Zen Garden. The same joy I felt in the poem. The joy of being alive and part of the earth, the realization of that connectedness.
Nicole Kristine Eidsvik, *Private Journals*

See Through My Eyes, Feel with My Skin

December 12

Dear Thay,

Our family has just returned from Vancouver where we attended a celebration of life for Lanette's daughter Nicole (Coley), who passed away from a rare form of bone cancer. The rhabdomyosarcoma was diagnosed three years ago, after she experienced unexplained pain in her back then discovered a suspicious lump on her groin. She's been courageously battling this relentless disease through intense rounds of chemotherapy and radiation, with a short remission in between—a tiny ray of hope throughout the dark periods of pain. Tragically, last year the cancer returned in full force, and this vibrant young beautiful girl passed away on November 22.

I feel like maybe you've already met Coley. In one of those rare and random moments, after being told that your public talk in Vancouver was sold out, a kind woman behind me in line offered me her tickets. Even though Coley was suffering with great pain at that time, she and Lanette were able to attend your dharma talk. A part of me was hoping she would get a chance to look into your eyes of love, like I did. I've prayed for her almost every day since she was diagnosed. I tried not to put expectations or boundaries on that healing, and yet deep down I was hoping for a miracle.

I remember a crystal-clear moment from when Coley was a baby, and I was babysitting. Coley was fussing and crying and just not able to settle. I held her and walked and walked, and rocked and rocked. Nothing seemed to soothe her. Finally, her weary body stopped fighting, and she relaxed into my arms. I remember looking into this tiny baby girl's eyes just before she drifted off to sleep and seeing her complete trust and innocence. It was a sacred moment of connection. I saw the "God Spark," a moment of oneness and grace. Like looking into your eyes Thay, it was an experience that cannot be put into words but is forever etched in my mind. I knew the light was strong in this new soul, but I didn't know how strong until her final battle with cancer.

From a young age, Coley seemed to have a close connection with God. She seemed an old, wise soul living in a young and energetic body. As a young girl, Coley loved to spend time in the tiny children's chapel at our church campgrounds. She wanted to be baptized as soon as she was old enough. She built and carefully tended a small Zen meditation garden in her backyard. Most of all, Coley loved to climb trees. She could be found fifty feet off the ground in an old cedar tree in the back alley, with her journal and her books. Even with cancer, Coley's light could not be contained. I'd like to believe that somehow this inner light got Coley and her family through her darkest moments, as she faced the relentless exhaustion and pain of the cancer that eventually took her life.

Both our boys were born in Vancouver, and our children are like brothers and sisters to each other. We share each other's joy and sorrow, so it's been important to visit Lanette and her family many times over these past three years. In each of my visits, I watched how life continued to unfold, even under the shadow of cancer, as if every day was even more precious. There was still laughter amidst the tears, thoughtfulness even in the midst of anger and frustration, family dinners nourishing body and soul, and calm, yet grief-stricken moments amidst the rush of work, and school, basketball games and practices, and the exhausting work of caring for a loved one. Each time I returned home, I had new prayers to pray.

On one of our last visits, I offered the sacrament we call the Laying on of Hands, a special prayer for the sick in our church, where a minister anoints the person in need with sacred oil, then says a prayer for comfort and healing. At one point Coley had been resistant to prayers, perhaps because she didn't want the spotlight, or perhaps because prayer had seemed to fail her when she needed it most. Yet at this particular time, there seemed to be an openness, and trust. Anointing her and placing my hands on her head, I found it difficult to find the right words to pray. The words did not flow. What flowed was the breath, along with spirit. I realized that in this space, words were no longer necessary. It was the love in our hearts and the willingness to simply offer all we carried— the doubt, the fear, the pain, the hope. There was a deep sense of being embraced by a love that is beyond our understanding, and the assurance of a love that allows us to let go of how we think things should turn out and simply trust in the mystery and uncertainty of life.

A month before Coley passed away, she and I visited one last time, and I shared what I could to help ease her pain, from breathing with her to teaching her some relaxation techniques. Would she like to receive some healing Thai yoga massage? I asked, and she slowly nodded her head. I believe in the power of ritual and symbolism, and intentionally creating sacred space, so I lit some candles and anointed her with oil of frankincense—the same oil given to the Christ child. I slipped a pink quartz meditation bracelet, infused with the energy of many months of my own prayers and meditation, onto her thin bony wrist.

As I gently massaged her, and as we both connected to the timeless rhythm of the breath, the image of a fussy baby settling came back into my mind. Coley opened her eyes briefly, and I saw those same ageless eyes, the eyes of God reflecting back the love that we are. I knew in that moment, despite her immense pain and suffering, that Coley knew that she was not her body, she was not the cancer, she was not her pain. She was already in touch with the part of her that was beyond pain, that was beyond birth, that was beyond death...timeless, eternal, and free.

Coley passed away with her family by her side in late November. That same day, a friend gave me *The Book of Awakening* by Mark Nepo. Mark has faced dark moments in his own battle with cancer, and the book has readings and meditations for each day of the year. I turned to the reading for that day: "I've learned that grief can be a slow ache that never seems to stop rising, yet as we grieve, those we loved mysteriously become more and more a part of who we are. In this way, grief is yet another song the heart must sing to open the gate of all there is."[7]

Nicole's celebration of life was held at beautiful Christ Church Cathedral in downtown Vancouver. The service began with singing. "Silent Night! Holy Night." The beautiful and poignant service was filled with songs and readings, poetry and personal stories—a tribute to the legacy of her young and courageous life.

I wonder if Coley had connected with you at some level, when she and Lanette went to your dharma talk at the Orpheum Theatre, in Vancouver. As we left the church, a homeless man with baggy pants and scruffy beard approached me, looking for spare change. Looking into his face, I saw the most beautiful eyes, not the hungry ghost eyes of street people who have lost hope, but tender compassionate eyes, like your eyes, like Coley's eyes, like the eyes of Christ. I didn't have much change on hand, but offered up a few coins, then glanced away for just a moment, and he was gone. It's as if he disappeared into thin air. Perhaps I have received my answer.

Touching the Hem of His Garment

The highest expression of the spirit is the one that opens us to the
Great Other in love and trust...This communion can be so intense
that the soul of the beloved is fused with the Lover in an experience
of non-duality. By grace we participate in God's being. Here the
human spirit is touching the hem of the Holy Spirit's garment.
Leonardo Boff, *Come, Holy Spirit*

December 18

Dear Thay,

As Christians, we celebrate this time before Christmas as Advent, a time
of waiting for the Christ to be born anew in our hearts. I'm thinking of
Mary, and the story of the angel visiting her as a young peasant girl,
telling her that she would become pregnant and give birth to the Christ
child. What faith she must have had to keep this secret gift of saving love
growing in her belly and her heart, and yet still face the doubts and fears
of rejection. Perhaps we are all like Mary, waiting to give birth to the
Christ or Buddha in our own hearts, despite the doubt and resistance
we may feel.

I am filled with both wonder and doubt from the depth of my encounter
with you. It's easy for the "doubting Thomas" in me to question the
experience. Yet the very real and visceral experience seems imprinted
in my cellular memory, reminding me of the "lightness" and love I felt
transmitted to me in that moment. In a flash, the powerful image that
came to me in that timeless moment of gazing into your eyes, returns. I
was that woman in the Bible story, that woman in the crowd, reaching
out to touch the hem of Christ's garment.

These stories are somehow embedded in my consciousness, perhaps
even from generations before. This story of the woman's encounter with
Jesus seems like an important story for me to unpack, to contemplate
deeply, as I look for the hidden meaning in my own life.

Many sincere Christian practitioners are embracing the ancient spiritual practice of Lectio Divina, a transformative way of reading sacred scripture—not as a way of information-gathering for debating who is right or wrong—but to slow down, to savour the words and phrases and images, and to meditate on its message for our own life. This kind of reading is reflective and prayerful, concerned with depth and receptivity, with feeling the story in the fertile ground of our own body and mind, as we seek to be formed more deeply in the body and mind of Christ. So, I have taken time to see how this woman's story in Luke 8:42-48 (NIV) lives in me.

As Jesus was on his way, the crowds almost crushed him. And a woman was there who had been subject to bleeding for twelve years, but no one could heal her. She came up behind him and touched the edge of his cloak, and immediately her bleeding stopped.

"Who touched me?" Jesus asked.

When they all denied it, Peter said "Master, the people are crowding and pressing against you."

But Jesus said, "Someone touched me; I know that power has gone out from me."

Then the woman, seeing that she could not go unnoticed, came trembling and fell at his feet. In the presence of all the people, she told why she had touched him and how she had been instantly healed. Then he said to her, "Daughter, your faith has healed you. Go in peace."

As always, I begin by bringing awareness to my body and breath. I feel the connection to my breath as an ancient symbol of spirit, connecting me to this woman who lived and breathed over two thousand years ago. As I sit in silence, my mind clears and I imagine the crowds pressing in on Jesus. I can see this woman following behind in the dust, trying to get closer to this rabbi who she has heard has healing in his hands. She has been bleeding for twelve long years, and no one seems to be able to help her.

Blood is symbolic of life in scripture. So, it is as if this woman's life force is flowing out of her, ebbing away. She hangs back in the crowd until her faith and her longing to be whole propel her forward, and she touches the hem of His garment. As she reaches out, Christ's life energy flows in. Jesus doesn't just heal her physically, but touches something alive in her soul.

As the Christ power flows into the woman's body, Jesus knows it. He asks his disciples "Who touched me?" This seems like a ridiculous question when so many people in the crowd are pressing in all around him. Yet it isn't just the touch of her hand on his garment that Jesus felt. He felt the "touch" of the faith in her heart, in his own heart. Jesus wants to see her eye-to-eye, face to face. He wants this woman to know that he knows. So he asks again, "Who touched me?" When she answers "It was I," he tells her, "Daughter, your faith has healed you. Go in peace." He speaks love and acceptance into her heart, and she knows she will never be the same again.

How has my "lifeblood" been flowing lately? Before I met you, dear Thay, my life had been flowing out of me, spinning out of control. It took my mom's journey through cancer and death to finally slow me down and remind me of what's most important in life. After she died, I made a vow to honour her memory by sustaining this slower, gentler way of being and loving. I wasn't sure how. Then, I met you. Like the woman in the story, I was changed and transformed through one holy sacred encounter. Like the woman in the story, I was hidden in the crowd, consumed by my own grief and lack of self-esteem. Then something catapulted me off my cushion. Perhaps it was a tiny seed of faith, watered by my own longing and naked need for God. Perhaps it was the powerful magnet of your loving presence. As your eyes caught mine, it was as if you had to work hard to get my attention. I could feel the strength of your penetrating gaze, like a laser beam blasting through the armouring around my heart. Then, when my heart was laid bare and you knew you had my complete and utter attention, your gaze softened, and your gentle smile melted what was left of my heart.

In the intensity of that moment, I knew there was no place that "I" could hide. I could feel the love of the Living Buddha, Living Christ pouring through your eyes into the hidden and wounded places of my soul. As your gaze continued to soften, I could see a reciprocal delight, as if we had just shared an intimate and sacred moment together, despite the crowd. I felt my whole body change, as if awakening and coming back to life. I didn't need to hear any words. They had already been written on my heart. "Your faith has healed you. Go in peace and be free."

CHAPTER 8

Healing the Past in the Present Moment

*An analogy for bodhicitta is the rawness of a broken heart.... This
continual ache of the heart is a blessing that when accepted fully
can be shared with all.*
Pema Chodron, *The Places That Scare You*

A Lazy Day of Mindfulness

January 4, 2012

Dear Thay,

How insightful you are to suggest to your students that we try to take one "lazy day" every week. You know the North American mind so well, with our tendency to dash from one place to another, from one long list of never-ending activities, our cell phones always ringing and beeping with an uninterrupted flow of phone calls, emails, and texts, and social media postings. It's so exhausting!

I have declared today, January 4, a lazy day for myself. It is a sabbath, a day of rest. This is a day I will spend offline, without the constant need to check emails or social media. It is a day to slow down and follow the gentle whisperings of my heart, to let all my goals and tasks sit quietly beneath my meditation cushion. It's not easy to plan a day like this; however, I don't start teaching my winter yoga classes until next week, so I can let go of the planning and scheduling for now, and simply trust in the insight that will arise from this day of doing nothing.

I feel like I have composed many letters to you in my mind. Some I have taken time to record in my journals. Others lie quietly, waiting for the right time to become words on a page. Today seems like one of those days when I can slow down, and allow the words the space they need to form into patterns and sentences that will speak to the questions of my heart.

You continue to be present in all of my thoughts and in everything I do and say. It is such a mystery to me. How can one fleeting moment in time make such a lasting imprint on my heart? I confess I'm not always mindful about staying in the present moment, as you teach. I find myself lost in daydreams, imagining private moments and conversations. I talk to you in my mind, like a child with an imaginary playmate, asking questions, telling you my heart's deepest, most intimate feelings.

Your picture is on my altar in my meditation room, where I light a candle invoking your light and presence every time I practice. As I gaze at this picture, it seems as if your eyes are looking deep into my soul again, and once more I am filled with your loving presence. Like a powerful magnet, my mind is drawn back to that mystical moment when our eyes met, and the deep love and compassion I saw in your eyes, so tender, so intimate, melting my heart, as our two hearts dissolved into one heart of inter-being. It is this oneness I still feel. It's as if I took a part of you back home with me. You are there not only in my sitting but also in my walking, my washing the dishes or vacuuming, in everything I do.

It is a divine mystery. You are right here, dear teacher, every step of the way, a light guiding me back home to myself. A phrase from one of your books, or a sentence from one of your online dharma talks, often speaks directly to my life. I have continued to practice with the gathas you gave at your retreat in Colorado. "Buddha is breathing, Buddha is sitting. Christ is the breathing, Christ is the sitting" often changes into "Thay is breathing, Thay is sitting. Thay is the breathing, Thay is the sitting." I feel as if you and the Buddha and the Christ are all somehow living and breathing in me. Somehow all this is transforming me at subtle levels I have yet to become aware of.

I have absolutely no idea how this divine love affair between us works. I have to feel and breathe my way, step by faltering step. I have read about other people's relationships with their teachers and gurus, but this love is beyond all the categories I've experienced. I am not a nun. I am not Buddhist. I am separated from you by thousands of miles and by the formality of your status as a respected Zen Master who is revered all around the world. Yet somehow I trust, whether through these letters, or through my practice, that there is a connection with you beyond my rational understanding. The seed of mindfulness and love you've planted in me continues to grow and blossom, even in the cold snow of a Canadian winter.

The Question of My Heart

I'm still not sure what mysterious force brought me up on stage with you to ask the "question of my heart" at the retreat in Vancouver. It is a question that is difficult to put into words. I'm not sure I could have asked it in front of eight hundred people either. It's a very personal and intimate question, and perhaps that's the nature of the deepest questions of our hearts. They can't always be put into words, to be neatly asked or answered. One question usually leads to a deeper, underlying question, like Buddhist koans that can't be grasped by the rational mind, and may take years of attention and practice to fully understand.

Yesterday was six months exactly to the day that my mother passed away, July 3, 2011. There is a sweet sadness with her memory, but no overwhelming grief. I have shed a few gentle tears, but there has been no torrent of tears. I find myself wondering, am I somehow repressing my grief? Shouldn't I be more grief-stricken that I'll never feel my mother's arms around me again?

My question has something to do with feeling versus repressing emotions. I can feel the sadness in my heart as a tender ache for all the ways I will miss my mother, but I wonder if there is a deeper grief waiting to be felt. Does grief peel away in layers, with different textures to be felt and explored? How do we know when we've peeled away the final layer? Maybe we never do. I read in one of your books that you still have feelings of sadness and despair for the ravage of wars and loss of students and friends in your homeland.

I feel as if I've lived a very easy and blessed life in many ways, although I've had my share of heartbreak and challenges. I was born into a family that certainly wasn't perfect, but my two brothers and I knew a kind of love that accepted us, and encouraged us to be our best, and to share our love with others. Doug and I have created our own family, passing on that same love to our two sons, as they grow from active boys into teenagers who think they already know everything! I have a healthy physical body nourished by wholesome vegetarian food, and a daily practice of yoga that grounds me to the earth, and helps me flow through the inevitable ups and downs of life. Sometimes I feel like I'm living a fairy tale life. I do not seem to suffer much, not compared to others. I watch the news and see the terrible injustices and atrocities taking place across the globe. How can I say that I suffer amidst the backdrop of so much unimaginable pain and tragedy? Yet I know we all have suffering, both individually and collectively. We "inter-are," so that mother in Africa crying for her young child who died of malnutrition is also in me. Can I let myself feel that?

Losing My Mother, Finding Myself

Even an old person, when he loses his mother, doesn't feel ready.
He too has the impression that he is not yet ripe, that he is suddenly
alone. He feels as abandoned and unhappy as a young orphan.
Thich Nhat Hanh, *A Rose for Your Pocket*

Dear Thay,
It's been less than one year since my mother was diagnosed with ovarian cancer. Like scenes from a movie, memories of this time are forever etched into my mind and heart. I can still hear the sound of her laboured breathing when we first arrived at the hospital in March, watching as

they removed two full bags of viscous fluid from her right lung. I can see the compassionate look in the doctor's eyes as she gave the diagnosis of stage IV ovarian cancer, a diagnosis we would have to repeat over and over again to my mother as her progressing Alzheimer's erased the memory of her diagnosis from the day before. I can still hear the heart-wrenching sobs and prayers I heard all night from her bedroom, as she spent her last night in her own home before moving to palliative care.

The next day we moved her into St. Michael's palliative care centre here in Lethbridge, so she could be close to me for whatever time she had left. In the busyness of my life, I was able to slow down and make space just to be with her through this difficult time. Even though it was hard to watch both her physical and emotional pain, there were also times of simply sitting quietly with her, as she shared many memories from her life. I listened to these stories with abiding love for the woman who has raised me from a babe in arms to being a mother now myself. Somehow I was able to listen without judgment, and without becoming overwhelmed.

Every night I would go home and practice Yoga Nidra, a practice of lying down meditation I have taught for many years. It is similar to the Plum Village practice of Deep Relaxation. I would lovingly bring attention to each part of my body, sending breath and healing energy, and allowing the layers of grief and sadness to be felt and to slowly dissolve. Often, I would fall asleep, and awaken with a few soft tears glistening in my eyes.

I continued to watch the terrible suffering that cancer wreaks on the body as I accompanied my mother on this inevitable journey. I held her hand and prayed as I watched the emotional suffering arise, as she let go little by little of everything and everyone she held dear. Somehow I could just be with all of this, even in my tired and grief-stricken state. My cousin Elizabeth said I was like a brick. Yet I felt more like a willow, planted firmly in the earth, able to bend and flow with the wind.

The tumour grew quickly, as the cancer cells had already spread to the lining of her stomach, and soon her belly became so distended, she looked as if she were pregnant. How strange, to walk into a maternity store to buy maternity pants meant to shelter new life, but which would instead shelter the very tumour that would take my mother's life. Slowly her body faded away to a frail shadow, skin on bone. Her three remaining sisters came to be with her. I watched them sit around her bed, and for a few moments caught a glimpse of the beautiful girls they once were as their now eighty-year-old bodies prayed and sang my mother into eternity.

I remember the look in my mother's ageless eyes as she said good-bye to my brother Don, before he left to go back home to Missouri, knowing they would never see each other again in this life. The very last picture taken, a few days before she passed, was with my eighteen-year-old son, Brendan, visiting, dressed in his graduation cap and gown. She knew she would not see him walk across the stage to receive his diploma, yet somehow the picture perfectly captures the love in her tired eyes.

Several days before she passed away, she started mumbling incoherently in her sleep. She then sat up and clearly said "There's Gerry, and he's holding my dress." Something in her knew that her time on this earth was short, and that somehow her husband and her God were beckoning to her from beyond. The bible talks about the "wedding garment" of Christ and getting ready to take on the "eternal body." Her faith allowed her to see and receive this new dress that would take her into eternal life.

The night before she passed away, I stayed in her room. She sometimes tried to get out of bed by herself, and I was afraid that she would fall. Lying in the darkness on a chair, I listened for the sound of her breath, and for the slightest rustle. I heard a slight creak and groan as she gripped the side rails that were supposed to prevent her from getting out of bed. Sure enough, she attempted to hoist herself up and over them, and I rushed to prevent her from falling on frail limbs that could no longer hold even her birdlike weight.

"I have to brush my teeth," she whispered in a weak raspy voice. I could have suggested waiting until morning, but something in me sensed that this was for her an important moment. I lowered the bars, then gently took her frail body into my arms. Slowly, I walked her to the bathroom, supporting her weight completely from behind. We found her toothbrush and toothpaste neatly packed in her bright pink butterfly cosmetic bag. I stood behind her, supporting her weight, and watched as she carefully squeezed the paste onto her brush. I watched her reflection in the mirror as she slowly and meticulously brushed the teeth she had brushed faithfully for over eighty years, as if she would need them for the next eighty. It was such a simple act, but in this moment, a sacred act.

Perhaps it is these simple daily acts done with loving care that make up the many moments of our life. This whole ritual touched me deeply. I did not know it would be the last time she would brush her teeth before taking her last breath the next day. I now smile at the thought that she would be reunited with my dad with pearly white teeth!

The next day was Sunday. Doug came to relieve me so I could get a bit of sleep. I came back in the afternoon and we both sat in silence, listening to the raspy sound of her slow and laboured breathing. We'd told her how much we loved her and that it was all right for her to finally let go. We sat and held her hand, occasionally wiping her brow or moistening her parched lips. There's something very tender and intimate about listening to someone breathing, and more acutely heartbreaking when they are close to death. At some point her breath began to slow, with long pauses in between. Finally, there was the long pause before her very last breath. There was a deep silence in that moment. It was both a sacred and ordinary moment, as the animating force of my mother's life left her body, yet could still be felt in the space and presence all around, and most of all in the very depths of our hearts.

As we left St. Michael's that day, we passed the table with a lamp that is turned on when a loved one departs. As I switched on the light, I read the words next to the lamp, by the great Bengali poet, Rabindranath Tagore: "Death is not extinguishing the light; it is only putting out the lamp because the dawn has come."

A Doll in the Closet

March 17

Today, St. Patrick's Day, would have been my mother's eighty-third birthday. There are no green balloons this year, and I find a flood of memories tying me back to her like the knot of brightly colored ribbons that held the balloons from last year. With misty eyes, I glance over at the doll sitting like a queen on a throne of pillows at the head of my bed. The doll belonged to my mother and accompanied me home after she passed away last year. Caitlin sits smiling at me with her brown eyes, her life-like body dressed in a frilly pink party dress with lacy pantaloons peaking out from underneath. I hear her whisper, "Pick me up and hold me."

I take Caitlin into my arms. Her weight feels like a real baby. Even her tiny hands and feet have life-like lines embedded into the skin, and fingers and toes that curl just like a baby's might. As I look into Caitlin's eyes and feel the weight of her body in my arms, the story of how this doll and my mother's life—and now mine—intertwine comes into focus.

As a young girl, my mother really never had a doll of her own. Life was very difficult for my grandmother and her seven daughters after my grandfather died. At the time, my mother, the youngest, was only two years old. There is a picture of my mother sitting on the dusty ground in front of an old farmhouse, holding a tattered stuffed bunny. It speaks to what I imagine the Dirty Thirties to be, and the dire circumstances that my mother and her sisters grew up in. Being the youngest, Mom always had hand-me-downs and nothing she could call her own. She also grew up without a father, and my grandmother was too busy working and trying to support her family to pay much attention to sweet little Patti.

Several years before my dad passed away in 2006, my mother was out shopping in a small gift store close to where she lived in Calgary.

Her eyes were drawn to a beautiful life-like doll and the little girl in her yearned for that doll she never had. She stood there admiring the doll but ninety dollars was way too frivolous, and how silly of her to buy herself a doll at the ripe age of seventy-five!

So my mother went home. Only that doll's beautiful face kept popping up in her memory. Finally, the little girl in my mother won out, and she decided she would go back and "look." How disappointed she was when she walked into the store and the doll was gone! My mother could have simply walked out of the store thinking the doll had been sold, and ignored that inner voice. Yet once again the little girl in her won out. Bravely, she went up to the store clerk and asked about that doll that had been sitting on a certain shelf. What a mixture of joy and relief when the store clerk smiled. "Is that the doll you're looking for?" the clerk asked with a twinkle in her eyes, pointing to a higher shelf. And there she was, the doll's life-like brown eyes still begging my mother to take her home.

My mother dutifully counted out the money as the store clerk carefully put the doll back into her original box, with the name Caitlin embossed in gold letters. Still, the little girl in my mother wasn't quite ready to be acknowledged.

Mom was a bit embarrassed to tell dad about her frivolous purchase, so she left Caitlin in her box in the trunk of the car until she could sneak the doll in and hide her away in a closet. Every so often when the house was empty, my mom would go downstairs, take the box out of the large plastic bag that concealed it, and just look at this beautiful doll. It was as if my mother was slowly peeling back the layers to find the little girl in her own heart. So, Caitlin patiently sat in her box in the dark basement closet, waiting to be opened and held, and brought fully into the light.

As I now hold this doll in my own arms, another memory bubbles up from one of the secret stories my mother told me before she died. This story is about a real baby, my older brother, Bryce. Bryce was my mother's first child, born premature. His tiny body had to be placed in an incubator to help him breathe and grow and get his strength. After his birth my mother stayed in hospital for a week, getting her own strength back, then innocently asked the doctor when she and her new baby could go home. The doctor was not very kind or understanding in his answer. "Mrs. Richards, I don't care when you go home, but you're not taking that baby with you!" My mother burst into tears, took one more lingering look at her precious newborn baby boy, and left for home with my father.

The hospital was a ways from where they lived, and my mom and dad only had one car. My mom ached to hold her new baby boy, but it wasn't possible for her to visit. Dad worked at the hospital during the day as a pharmacist, and would go and look in on baby Bryce. Surrounded by a sea of bassinets filled with other babies, Bryce did not get held much for the three long weeks he was in hospital. When my mom and dad finally got to bring baby Bryce home from the hospital, my mother noticed that the skin on his tiny heels was red and raw from kicking in his bassinet. She never forgave herself. She kept this guilty secret most of her life, and always wondered what effect it had on Bryce and his life. Yet time and the events of our life have a way of healing, if we let it.

Somehow I feel like my mother's yearning for a doll she never had as a young girl was inextricably connected to a baby she never held as a new mother. I don't think my mom ever told my dad about the doll hidden in their basement. It wasn't until years after my dad died that my mother finally mentioned her doll to me, and even then, she felt a bit silly about her purchase. I gently asked if I could see this doll, and so down the stairs we went, to take her out of the closet.

There was Caitlin, still entombed in her original box. Under my mother's trembling gaze, I unwrapped the delicate tissue paper, opened the clear cellophane on the box, then finally cut the plastic ties that imprisoned Caitlin to her cardboard backing. As I gently placed the weight of this life-like baby doll in my mother's arms, I could sense the layers of my mother's life peeling away, revealing a young mother who never forgave herself for not being able to hold her newborn son, and farther back, to a girl who once yearned for a doll that would somehow take the place of the father she had lost to cancer. It was a profound moment of healing outside of time and space.

After finally being released from her prison to the light of day, Caitlin sat for a few years on my mother's bed, propped up between the pillows. She travelled down to Lethbridge with my mother when she grew ill, and was there in the room at St. Michaels when she passed away. Caitlin now sits on my bed, a reminder of the deep healing that was taking place in my mother's heart, and the yearning we all have to simply love and be loved. I think my mother was slowly learning to listen to her heart in preparation for her final journey. So, despite the worries, despite all the sleepless nights, despite the memory loss, despite the battle with cancer, God was working out the miracle of healing at a deep and profound level we couldn't always see.

I too, am learning to breathe and peel back the more intricate, subtle layers of suffering and joy that are inevitable parts of life. I am learning to trust and be patient, slowly living my way into my own answers.

PART 3

Re-igniting the Flame

*...at one point he glanced at her, caught her gaze,
and something passed between them. She was thunderstruck;
an energy and vibration filled her whole body. Her sight opened
and she saw his true form as light and fire and truth, and a love
such as she had never known welled up in her.*

Tau Malachi,
Living Gnosis: A Practical Guide to Gnostic Christianity

CHAPTER 9

We Meet Again

21-DAY RETREAT, 2012: THE SCIENCE OF THE BUDDHA.
PLUM VILLAGE, FRANCE

Sleeping Under the Bodhi Tree

June 1

Dear Thay,

It feels like such a long journey from the "awakening of my heart" in Vancouver to finally arriving at Plum Village. It's been nine months since that moment with you that completely changed the trajectory of my life; nine months of wondering, nine months of dreaming, nine months of anticipating. What will it be like to look in your eyes once more? I have followed the longing of my heart, and it has led me here to your home, an ocean away from mine, yet in some ways as close as my very own breath.

Doug and I will be celebrating our twentieth wedding anniversary this year, on June 27. Since I was already registered for this retreat, we decided to celebrate by making the trip to France together. We arrived in the whirlwind of Paris twelve days ago, taking in the dazzling sights and sounds of the City of Light, in sharp contrast to some of the magnificent cathedrals that seem to contain hundreds of years of silence and yearning for God. From Paris, we took a train down to Nimes, exploring the ancient Roman ruins and architecture of that area, then the beautiful rugged Cevennes mountains with vast views of the valleys. Finally, we explored the beautiful Dordogne area with a day at the famed Grotte de Lascaux, the underground caves discovered in 1940 with cave drawings said to be over 17,000 years old. From museums and cathedrals in Paris, to Roman coliseums and aqueducts, to cave drawings painted by ancient peoples, I am struck by the fluidity of time converging into this moment.

Finally, after following roads that meander and twist through vineyards and sleepy southern villages, we arrive at New Hamlet (thank goodness for GPS!) When I registered for this retreat in February, I had no idea that Plum Village consisted of three separate hamlets or monasteries that were so spread out: Upper Hamlet, Lower Hamlet and New Hamlet.

At New Hamlet we park by a wrought iron fence, then follow a path leading past a small lotus garden to a group of stone buildings. Nuns in long brown robes are bustling about in a mindful way, directing us to the registration area, where we find other bewildered-looking travelers. This is an international retreat with over a thousand people from all over the world, and I hear snippets of French, German, Italian, and Vietnamese. To my surprise, the couple behind us are from Calgary, Alberta, only 200 km from my own home in Lethbridge. I wonder about the life stories and circumstances that have brought all of us together at this particular time and place. You, dear Thay, seem to be the magnet that attracts us.

After finishing the registration process I am told that I will not be staying in the main part of New Hamlet, but in a converted farmhouse called "Gate House," just a short walk away. When the tiny Vietnamese nun doing the registration notices the size of my suitcase, she looks a bit worried and in a shy voice she asks "Will you be all right carrying your suitcase there yourself?" When I smile and say "Yes thanks, my husband has a rental car," her eyes light up. "Would you mind giving other people a ride as well?" she asks. I glance at Doug, knowing that he has a long journey still to drop the car off at the rental office, and make his train to Paris. With only a slight hesitation, he smiles and says "of course." That's Doug. That's the nature of true love.

We stuff three more tired travelers, plus backpacks and suitcases, into the tiny rental car and drive to the rambling farmhouse. From the outside, it looks a bit rundown, but we unload, and Doug helps me lug my suitcase up creaky stairs to the second floor, where we find my room and meet Ann from Thailand. Ann will be my roommate for the next twenty-one days. Our room is simple, stark, with twin beds and a side table, a small open bookcase along the wall for our belongings, and one wooden chair. I ask where the washrooms are, and Ann points back down the stairs. There are twelve women sharing one bathroom! Just breathe, I remind myself.

I walk back to the car with Doug to say good-bye. Looking into his eyes, the love I see reminds me of you, dear Thay. We embrace and I feel his strength and the depth of his love that allows me to follow this spiritual path of my heart. I watch tenderly as he slowly backs out of the gravel driveway. With one last wave, the car disappears. As I look out at the field in front of the house, I feel a twinge of loneliness. I wish he could stay too, but we've already left our teenage boys at home, alone, for two weeks. Five weeks would be pushing it. And, besides, the true spiritual path is often lonely, taking us to unfamiliar places. I trudge up to my room, and see a sign on my door that says Bodhi. I smile. The Buddha was said to have attained enlightenment under the Bodhi tree. I wonder what enlightenment I'll receive here?

Be Like the Lotus Leaf

Be like the lotus leaf. Drops of water glide off the lotus leaf without being absorbed by it. We aspire to be like the lotus leaf, so that our sensual desire glides off us, and we keep our equanimity.
Thich Nhat Hanh, *Fidelity*

June 2
Dear Thay,
Today is a day to settle in and adjust to our schedule and surroundings. I've taken time to explore the beauty of New Hamlet, starting at the bell tower, then walking slowly through the stately rows of plum trees, then making my way up the hill to enjoy the view of the gently rolling hills and farmhouses in the distance. As I gaze at the peaceful scene below, I wonder what the next twenty-one days will bring. Will I have the chance to look into your loving eyes again? I am filled with anticipation, but also

nervous. Will I feel that vast expansive sense of love again in my heart, or will I be disappointed? Do I have too many expectations? "Breathing in I am calm, breathing out I release."

Wandering back down the hill, past the meditation hall, I find myself sitting by the lotus pond. Although there are no blossoms yet, the pond is blanketed with greenery, full of unlimited life and possibility. The morning sun is reflecting off the dew drops glistening on the smooth broad surface of the large green leaves. The drops are like tiny diamonds reflecting the light of the sun in all directions. I close my eyes and listen to a symphony of sounds: the low thrum of the frogs croaking, the melodious songs of birds. The pond is so alive with life. I can feel it in my body. I open my eyes and my gaze falls on one solitary frog. A dewdrop on his tiny chest has caught the sun at just the right angle, and sparkles each time his tiny heart beats. I can feel my own heart beating, my own heart shimmering. We are both tiny sparks of light glistening in and out of eternity.

The Mere Exchange of a Glance

Two people on this earth who love and understand each other
deeply do not require words or signs. The mere exchange of
a glance is enough to communicate everything that matters...
That must be the kind of love unfolding between the soul and her
Beloved in this kind of vision. Without the soul knowing how, the
two lovers gaze directly at one another's face.
St. Teresa of Avila, *The Book of My Life*

June 3

Dear Thay,

Today after early morning meditation and breakfast at New Hamlet, we all board a bus for the thirty minute drive to Lower Hamlet, where you are giving the first dharma talk of this retreat. There is a loud hum of voices talking excitedly until someone invites the sound of the bell, and we settle into the silence of "bus riding meditation" together. I sit quietly observing my breath, watching the scenery outside with its rolling hills and rows of vineyards. I am filled with the quiet anticipation of seeing you once again.

At Lower Hamlet, I follow the throng of people moving towards what I hope is the meditation hall. Once there, I remove my shoes, hoping they won't get lost among all the others, then carefully pick my way through the long lines of meditation cushions to a place close to the front. With another thirty minutes until the dharma talk begins, I sit on my cushion quietly breathing, trying to slow down the nervous questions in my mind. You have hundreds of thousands of students all over the world. How can you possibly recognize them all? I wonder if you will even know me. I feel pretty silly and self-absorbed, like a nervous schoolgirl, waiting for her first date.

The room begins to settle, and finally the small bell sounds. We all stand, hands together at our hearts, watching our beloved teacher enter the hall, imprinting his love with every step he takes. With the agility of a much younger man, you sit down on your cushion, then motion for everyone to sit down.

We start with silent meditation and, as is my practice at home, I begin by repeating the word "Beloved" silently in my mind, as a way of connecting to you and the vast love you embody. "Be..." as I inhale, "Lo...ved..." as I exhale, the syllables dropping into my heart centre like gently falling rain. With each breath, I settle into the support of this beloved community.

You start the way you start every dharma talk, stating the date and the place: "Good morning, dear sangha. Today is Sunday, June third, 2012. We are in the Assembly of Stars Meditation Hall, Lower Hamlet for the 21-Day Retreat with the theme "The Science of the Buddha." You look around, and your dazzling smile lights up the room. What a joy to see you so close and be in your presence once more. I still can't believe I'm here. All your students love you so much. It seems that I'm not the only one infatuated with you. Your love and wisdom and Zen power touches something very deep in all of us.

At one point you walk out into the sea of meditation cushions and stop a short space away from me. Hardly daring to breathe, my eyes are glued to your face. I watch as your eyes seem to flicker and dart razor fast to me, somehow acknowledging me, then taking the whole sangha in again. It was so subtle. If I had blinked, I would have missed it. It felt like somehow you can recognize us by our inner energetic quality, and not just our outer appearance. Is it like this for all of your students and disciples? How can you possibly recognize us all? It sounds so crazy. Perhaps I'm just completely deluded in my thinking. Yet I cannot deny the truth of my mystical experience with you last summer, and the love that has set my heart on fire. This is mystery, beyond my rational mind to understand.

The monastics start chanting "Avalokiteshvara, the Buddha of Compassion." You invite us to get in touch with our own suffering, then send the energy of prayer to our loved ones. The chanting is so deep and beautiful. The woman beside me is quietly sobbing. I am peaceful and quiet and tender, but no tears. Perhaps I'm not looking deeply enough. I don't seem to have much suffering. I certainly struggle with self-identify, always judging and comparing myself to others. I seem to have been practicing for a very long time simply to accept myself as I am. Where does this come from? Does it come from me, or does it come from my mother, who struggled with her own self-image? Is it linked to generations of women unable to be their true selves in a society where the wisdom of the feminine is repressed and not valued? How do I heal this? Another question to meditate on. Perhaps I'll get more insight during this retreat.

Can You Read My Mind?

Our mind of love may be buried deep in our store consciousness,
under many layers of forgetfulness and suffering. The teacher's
role is to help us water it, to help it manifest.
Thich Nhat Hanh, *Cultivating the Mind of Love*

June 4

Dear Thay,

Yesterday in walking meditation, you led us through a stately line of poplar trees into the quiet depth of the forest with a small stream trickling through it. It's a true miracle that so many people can walk so quietly through the forest when they are mindful of their steps. I think Mother Earth must have been happy to receive all of our loving steps. We crossed a tiny bridge, then wound our way out of the forest and into a clearing, where you stopped and gracefully sat on a mat provided by your attendant. A rustling of jackets and mats and backpacks, and soon we all found a place to stand or sit, to enjoy in silence the peaceful energy. A few people took their cameras out as well, quietly taking advantage of this moment to be so close to you.

I remembered the time in our walking meditation in Vancouver, when I raised my camera to take a picture of you. I put it away when I realized that I was mindlessly treating you as an object. Yet now, I really wanted to have a picture of you to take home from Plum Village. I took out my camera, and breathed into the place where I feel you, in my heart centre. Then, silently in my mind, I asked you if I could take your picture. To my utter surprise, you turned and looked directly at me, with a knowing look in your eyes, and a beautiful smile on your face. With one click, this image was saved on my camera and engraved on my heart.

Today you start your dharma talk at Upper Hamlet, again with meditation. There is something very powerful about sitting quietly in meditation together with over a thousand people. The field of concentration feels very strong, and I imagine all this peaceful energy rippling out into the world. You begin your talk by saying "This sitting is like sitting under the Bodhi tree. Meditation gives us the time to look deeply." You glance briefly at me. I am staying in the Bodhi Room at Gatehouse. Do you have these secret messages for everyone listening to your talks—a word here, a glance there, a silent transmission of love and wisdom from your heart to ours? This feeling that you can somehow read my mind, leaves me feeling vulnerable, exposed. It's like you can see beyond the mask I wear to the thoughts and feelings I hide from others, and even things buried deep in my unconscious mind.

After your dharma talk, once again you lead us in walking meditation, this time winding down the side of the hill by your hut at Upper Hamlet, then following a path through the forest until we come to the foot of a grassy hill. As I follow the mass of people up the hill, I realize that among the trees at the top are sixteen stone Buddhas, silent sentinels looking out over the vast valley below. You stop to sit in their midst, and we all find a place to sit scattered among the statues. Perhaps we are all Buddhas-to-be. I find a place to sit close to you. Yet this time I am so nervous, my thoughts are scattered like the leaves shaking in the trees above us. How does one be completely present with a wise teacher who seems to know your every thought?

This is nothing like the first time I looked in your eyes, in Vancouver. This time my self-consciousness and judgment gets in the way. With no place to hide, my heart turns to stone. Like the rough stone Buddhas on the hill, your stern Zen master face reflects the closing off of my own heart.

I feel self-absorbed. I'm so confused about how this relationship with you works, and how to act in your presence. I know I'm over-thinking. I simply need to return to my breath and practice, and trust that everything will be revealed in time. A lot can happen in twenty-one days, or then again, perhaps nothing at all. It all depends on me, and my willingness to shed the protective walls I've built around my heart.

CHAPTER 10

The Practices Ripen

A Practice of Falling in Love with Your True Self

June 5

Dear Thay,

Sister Trai Nghiem has asked me if I would teach yoga during the early morning exercise time here at New Hamlet. I smiled and said yes, although yoga is so much more than exercise. It is a spiritual practice, a way of breathing and sensing and feeling the oneness of body, mind, and spirit. Yoga not only stretches our body, but opens our mind to a more spacious awareness. One of my first yoga teachers, Jennifer Steed, said "Yoga is a practice of falling in love with your true self." Indeed, that has been my experience, and somehow it has led me to you.

I am a bit nervous teaching here, and as usual my inner critic and judge show up. Before I start, I take a few moments to breathe, and to invite you to teach with me. We start the class with the sound of the bell. Somehow you are here teaching with me. Your presence, your words intertwined with mine, seem to flow effortlessly from my lips. I integrate your "Joy of Meditation" gathas into some of the postures and movements. You often use these to teach children how to be mindful and to use their imaginations to become a mountain, a flower, water, and space. Like most children's games or stories, the gathas seem to work for adults as well.

Breathing in, Breathing out. Feel each breath as a precious gift of life. Let yourself move with the rhythm of life. Feel the still point of the cycle of breath.

Breathing in, I see myself as a mountain, breathing out I feel solid. Feel your roots reaching deep into the soil of Mother Earth through your feet, then take that stability into other postures.

Breathing in, I see myself as still water. Breathing out, I reflect all that is. Feel the qualities of water in you, the flow of the ocean, the trickle of a stream, the stillness of the mountain lake, reflecting perfectly the love that you are.

Breathing in, I see myself as space. Breathing out I feel free. Feel the space in your muscles and joints. Feel the space in your mind and your heart. Feel the space in every single cell of your body.

We end with the posture of savasana, the corpse pose, resting and surrendering our body and practice back to the earth, symbolically dying to who we think we are, so we can awaken to the vast love that we already are.

By the Light of the Full Moon

June 6

Dear Thay,

Your practice of Listening to the Bell is growing in me. You teach this as a way of stopping and coming back to our selves. Now, every time I hear a bell, whether in the meditation hall, or the dining hall, or the deep resonant sound of the morning and evening bells from the bell tower, my mind and body are trained to stop what I'm doing and simply come back to the present moment through my very own breath. Yet the practice is so much deeper than just stopping. I especially love the sound of the large bowl-shaped bells in the meditation hall. When I'm really still, I can feel my whole body lightly vibrating. In your dharma talk, you said that we should listen with our whole body, like every single cell is listening. I love that description. My cells are tingling. My whole body is shimmering.

There was a full moon shimmering last night. It was the fifth full moon, so we celebrated it as the Buddha's birthday and enlightenment. We all walked up to the top of Plum Hill at New Hamlet, with its stunning view of the valley below, but the moon was shy and eluded us. Later, we finally snuck a view of it from the yard around Gate House. In Buddhism, gates symbolize the liminality that marks the transition between the mundane and the sacred. Perhaps the moon is a gate for us. The silvery orb seemed to light up the whole skyline, shining Buddha's light of wisdom into all our hearts. Carmen was playing her flute, and it felt like the moon was Krishna seducing us into the fullness of Divine Love. I think of your gatha, based on the words of our ancestral teachers, in *The Blooming of a Lotus*:

Buddha is the cool moon, crossing the sky of utter emptiness.

The lake of the mind of beings quietens, the moon reflects beautifully in it.[8]

Buddha is Breathing, Christ is Sitting, Nobody's Here

June 7

Dear Thay,

Yesterday you used the practice of "Buddha is breathing, Buddha is sitting" in your dharma talk as a way to realize "non-self." This is the practice you transmitted at the retreat at Estes Park, Colorado just after the retreat in Vancouver. I felt the practice truly resonate in my heart, and knew I had found my practice. I have been practicing every day, although sometimes I substitute the Christ, and often "Thay." *Thay is breathing, Thay is sitting. Thay is the breathing, Thay is the sitting. I am the breathing, I am the sitting. There is only the breathing, There is only the sitting. No one is breathing, No one is sitting. Peace is the breathing, Joy is the sitting.*

It feels like I am slowly dissolving the "me" I think I am, to become the love beyond the boundaries of Buddha and Christ, and you and me.

I watch you very closely during your dharma talks. I don't want to miss a single nuanced word, look, or gesture. When you talk about this practice, you seem to be looking right at me. I feel a soft energy in my heart, and can stay focused both on the words and the feeling of the Buddha or Christ breathing in me.

It's not quite as strong as in Vancouver, more like the quiet, soft energy of a butterfly fluttering its wings. Your messages are very subtle. I have to be mindful and listen carefully. Yet still I doubt, and wonder if it's just my imagination. Even so, you don't give up. You keep sending me subtle Zen messages, patiently reminding me of who I really am (or who I am not!)

Another one of my daily practices is to repeat the "Divine Light Invocation," as taught by Swami Radha,[9] a disciple of Swami Sivananda of Rishikesh. Part of the invocation is to imagine oneself filling with light then holding others in that same light. This is the way I pray. I don't pray with words, not anymore. Instead, I take time to visualize the people in my life, animals and plants, and our dear planet in the light. My meditation room faces east, so quite often I receive the light of the rising sun, feeling the warmth on my face and skin. In the middle of your dharma talk, you spoke about the lotus opening to the sunlight, and how powerful meditation on light is. Once more, you looked at me with that beautiful smile that melts my heart, as if to say "I see your Light, my dear."

Today in our early morning meditation, we imagined ourselves as a five-year-old child. I could see my freckled face framed by a cute pixie cut, and our house at Lindsay Drive with the double garage and the swing set in the back. I wondered if I could send love and wisdom to my five-year-old self. You said "In the Ultimate dimension, there is no coming or going, no after no before, no birth no death, no beginning or end." Sounds like Zen talk to me. It's not something I can understand with my rational mind, but I could feel my five-year-old heart in my fifty-year-old body. I felt her joy swinging on the swings, and skipping down the sidewalk. Maybe that's what you mean by "no after, no before." I feel a kind of timelessness where my five-year-old self is here with my fifty-year old-self. Perhaps I can even feel my mother alive in me.

Growing in Grace, Learning by Insight

In Buddhism we speak of emancipation or salvation by means
of insight, not by grace. Yet insight is a kind of grace.
Thich Nhat Hanh, *Awakening of the Heart*

June 8
Dear Thay,
It is a Question and Answer dharma talk with you this morning. My mind returns to the strong urge I felt to rise and ask a question in Vancouver. I was mysteriously drawn closer to you, to receive your gaze of love that catapulted me into this divine love affair. I don't feel the need to get up this morning. My mind is at peace, and I have no burning questions that I want to ask in front of a thousand people. You seem to be able to answer the questions of my heart in silence.

This morning, I am seated in the front row, right across from you in your direct line of sight. I am content to simply bask in your peaceful, loving presence. I watch as a young slender woman gets up and pranams, bowing at your feet as is the custom in India at the feet of the Guru. She begins her question by looking directly at you and saying "I love you Thay." How brave she is to profess her love in front of all these people. Part of me wishes I could be that brave and vulnerable. Can you feel my love, Thay, this love that is beyond words or concepts? Do you need my words, or just my heart?

The young woman goes on to ask a question about how to deal with the superiority and inferiority complex. You answer with your usual Zen master wisdom. "It is not just the eyes that see things. Eyes are only one of the conditions for seeing. We also need nerves, cells, etc. Every thought or feeling you have is produced by your whole body, as well as your ancestors' bodies. You part cipate as well. We are together, always together. There is no separation at all".

I was close enough to see your eyes sparkling with love as you said this. My own eyes sparkled back.

I keep breathing out the love from my heart to you as the questions and answers continue. My mind floats back to the vividness of the moment of meeting your loving gaze. In my mind, I sent you my gratitude for what I call your "Gift of Grace." Not long after that, when you were answering someone's question, you made the comment that Buddhists don't believe in the concept of grace, that insight comes from deep looking. You said "Do not look at salvation as grace but as understanding, prajna. We are saved from suffering and fear, not by grace, but by the fruits of meditation, the practice of looking deeply."

What exactly is grace? Coley, in her young wisdom, even with her body racked with cancer, said that small kindnesses from others while waiting for chemo treatment, or just appreciating the reflection of sunlight on the wall in front of her, were tiny moments of grace. To me, grace is those flashes of insight or healing when we open up to the mystery in the moment. Often unexpected or unsought, it is those moments when we let go of control, those moments when we look deeply or see differently. Perhaps grace and insight are both the fruits of mindfulness and deep looking. Maybe the grace of your gaze is the same as the fruit of my insight.

Sharing From Our Hearts

The sangha is invited to come back to our breathing, so that our collective energy of mindfulness will bring us together as one, going as a river with no more separation.
Let the whole sangha breathe as one body, chant as one body, listen as one body, and transcend the boundaries of a delusive self, liberating from the inferiority complex, the superiority complex and the equality complex.
Opening Practices, *Plum Village*

June 9

Dear Thay,

I've been at Plum Village for a full week now. I can feel myself slowing down, taking mindful steps from Gatehouse to New Hamlet, feeling the aliveness of the trees, the birds, and the rich bouquet of wildflowers that dot the fields. As my steps slow down, I can feel my body softening and relaxing, releasing tension I wasn't even aware of. The rough edges of my thoughts have smoothed out, and even the lines on my face have softened. Perhaps I really am becoming that five-year-old girl I used to be! Yet I still have conflicting feelings, of both inferiority and superiority. My ego, my discriminating mind, always wants to compare myself with others, to judge, to feel better than or less than. How does one go about healing this?

Yesterday I shared in our dharma family group that I don't seem to struggle with strong feelings that overwhelm me. I've always been a gentle, even-minded person, and with fifteen years of yoga and meditation, I can look back and see how I've been able to let a lot of the seeds of anger and over-reacting go before they had a chance to explode. I have also lived a comfortable and blessed life in Canada, a country of wealth and opportunities not enjoyed by most people around the world. I was given a good start, being born into a family with parents who loved me, and knew how to express that love. They had a faith in God that, although somewhat rigid, gave me a foundation for exploring and being open to other faiths.

These seeds of love have sprouted in my own family, with a husband who looks at me with eyes of love that reflect my own. Our sons, Brendan and Andrew, are slowly growing into thoughtful young men, although they still struggle to find out who they are in a world that is speeding up, consuming people as fast as it is consuming food, and clothes, and social media, and alcohol, and drugs, and sex, and money, and ultimately, our planet. How can our younger generation find themselves in a world that has forgotten that it takes a global village to raise a child?

With over a thousand people at this retreat, it's easy to feel like a small fish in an ocean. It's helpful in the afternoons to sit down with our smaller dharma families to share about our own lives and experiences. Our dharma family is very lucky to be guided by Sister Chân Không, your dear friend and disciple from your earliest years in Vietnam. In her book, *Learning True Love: Practicing Buddhism in a Time of War*, she tells her own story of meeting you and working together for your people and advocating for the end of the war. Occasionally she has shared snippets of stories about your life together in Vietnam. I listen carefully to every word from the depths of my heart, and it seems as if there is a direct transmission of your love through hearing these precious details of your life. I often wonder what it would be like to be able to sit down and share a cup of tea with you, and hear these stories directly from you. Perhaps listening to Sister Chân Không is as close as I can get.

In our dharma group, I have heard stories of terrible suffering, from the traumas of abuse and alcoholism, to the loneliness and despair of sickness and poverty. As I listen to these heart-breaking stories with my own heart, I feel like I really have not suffered much. My own problems seem quite inconsequential in the face of the suffering of others. Yet can one truly compare how one experiences suffering? I know there are still seeds of suffering in me. How can I look more deeply at these in order to dig them up?

What about feelings and emotions? My practice has provided me with a deep sense of peace and equanimity amidst the changing circumstances of my life. At times, though, I wonder if I am repressing something. Perhaps we all repress to some degree. What exactly is the difference between equanimity, the ability to be with whatever arises, and repressing or being detached from one's feelings? These are deep questions to plant in the soil of my meditation practice.

Sometimes in my meditation practice, my heart feels so tender and open. Other times, it seems to close when I'm too busy or not willing to be fully present to whoever or whatever is right in front of me. I wonder if it's possible always to be open, to live with a completely unbounded heart, like you, like the Christ, like Buddha. If we can stay open to our own pain, can we stay open and compassionate to the pain of others? Perhaps there is no "other." Maybe that's the whole point.

I do tend to overthink and analyze too much. At the same time, I aspire to an open heart no matter what I'm going through. I know I need to look more closely at my doubts and insecurities. I have a tendency to want to please other people. I don't like conflict. I can be easily influenced by other people's opinions and expectations. Yet I'm slowly learning to stand firmly in the wisdom and insight that arises from my own practice. You saw that in me, and mirrored it back.

CHAPTER 11

Secrets Whispered
To My Heart

*If we take me out of you, then you would not be able to manifest
as you are manifesting now. If we take you out of me, I would not
be able to manifest as I am manifesting now. We cannot manifest
without one another. We have to wait for each other in order
to manifest together.*
Thich Nhat Hanh, *Inside the Now*

I Am You, and You Are Me

June 10

Dear Thay,

In your dharma talks you seem to have the capacity to talk and transmit
knowledge at so many different levels, from complicated Buddhist
philosophy to simple stories. Without notes, you speak effortlessly on
Buddhist concepts such as the Four Noble Truths, the Five Aggregates,
the Six Paramitas, The Seven Factors of Awakening, the Noble Eight-Fold
Path, internalism, annihilism, liberation, emancipation, reincarnation...
until my mind is so full, it needs a vacation. The theme of this retreat is
"The Science of the Buddha," and you've been making a connection
between conventional dualistic truth and Newtonian science, and
ultimate non-dual truth and quantum physics. Whether you're speaking
to scientists or shamans, Buddhists or Christians, monastics or children,
it feels as if you communicate with each person in whatever way they
will best understand.

Yet it is the silent language of love that speaks most to my heart.

Today you gave a deep dharma talk that touched on themes such
as the relationship between suffering and happiness, emptiness, and

the nature of non-locality. I was sitting close to the middle in the third row of cushions, feeling very quiet and settled in my heart centre. You were speaking about the separation most people feel when they bow or stand in front of the Buddha. You taught that we have to remove the obstacle between our self and the Buddha, or any enlightened being. Living beings and the Buddha are not different. We should not be stuck in the idea that the Christ is eternal and we are mortal. We all have the capacity to awaken to the Living Buddha or Living Christ in our self and in each other.

Slowly, I'm beginning to understand that when you have a message or teaching you really want me to get, you turn and look directly at me. This time was no different. You turned and looked at me as you said "Thay is non-local. I am here and I am everywhere. I am you and you are me." This timeless message of "inter-being" is what you seem to be teaching me through this mystical relationship. I know this message isn't just for me. I'm sure each person in the meditation hall receives it according to his or her own level of understanding. And yet once more you bypassed my head and went straight to my heart. Both your words and the energy that are transmitted seem to be an answer to all the questions I've had about you and our relationship--and a confirmation of what I already know in my heart. You continue to reveal yourself at deeper and subtler levels, if I simply surrender and let go of overthinking or trying too hard.

I feel that same sense of spaciousness I felt with you in Vancouver. Slowly, I walk back to the bus back to New Hamlet. There is a low hum of conversation, but I don't want to talk. I only want to be with the quiet energetic presence of you in my heart.

As I gaze out the bus windows at the passing vineyards and rolling hills, I have a sense that you are transmitting all of your knowledge, perhaps the entire lineage of your wisdom, as if there might not be much time left. It feels as if you are trying to awaken as many of us as you can before you leave your body. It is such a precious and sacred time to be with you, and receive the teachings. I want to be an empty vessel to receive all that you have to pour into my waiting heart.

A Love Letter on Lazy Day

June 11

Dear Thay,

Today is another "Lazy Day," as you call it, at the monastery. It is a day to let go of following the usual retreat schedule, and simply follow our heart's desire, listening deeply, letting the world unfold exactly as it is. It is like a sabbath or a desert day in the Christian tradition, a day to be quiet and attend to our inner life. Some people are uncomfortable with not having a schedule to follow, or spending time by themselves. They leave the monastery to enjoy a latte in the village. Although I'm tempted by the latte, I want to stay closer to you, and keep nourishing this inner silence that seems to be growing in the depths of my heart.

I enjoy the luxury of sleeping in a bit, then go to meditate on my own in the Buddha Hall. It is dark and quiet, with only a few candles burning, their shadows dancing on the rough texture of the old stone walls. Like the cathedrals I'd visited in Paris, the hall feels full of ancient mystery. I sit, and bring my attention to the familiar rise and fall of my breath. The words "Christ is breathing, Christ is sitting" begin to flow silently with each breath. I smile at the thought of the Christ breathing and meditating in a Buddhist monastery. I think both the Christ and Buddha would smile too. I look up for a moment and see a picture of Christ on the altar smiling back at me.

I sink into a peaceful meditative state, feeling like the Christ consciousness is truly present in me (and the Buddha too.) Sometimes, after I get up off my cushion I wonder if I'm meditating correctly. At our dharma sharing, people talk about feelings like anger, or fear, or sadness that come up for them when they meditate. Negative feelings like this never seem to come up while I am meditating. I get bored or distracted sometimes, but most times I seem to be able to sink into a peaceful sense of abiding. I've heard the term "spiritual by-passing," and wonder if I'm using meditation to avoid dealing with feelings that might lie beneath the surface of my conscious mind. How does one become conscious of these hidden feelings, or more subtle suffering? Perhaps my practice is to simply stay present as these feelings arise in daily life. Maybe our daily life is our most important practice.

What exactly is this seed of love you have planted in my heart? Or, was the love already there, and you simply touched it, like a match to dry tinder? Like a lovesick schoolgirl, my mind keeps returning to that moment our eyes met, to anchor it in memory. That moment has become a touchstone that connects me to your deep well of love anytime, anywhere. I get lost in daydreams of you, and imagine what it would be like to spend time with you walking in the forest, or just quietly sipping tea together. I've been secretly hoping that I might meet you when walking by myself at the top of Plum Hill here at New Hamlet. I look for you everywhere. Ever since I met you last summer, I've been dreaming of coming to Plum Village. At first I was nervous to be in your presence again. I could not calm my mind, which was constantly jumping from one thought to another. Since you seem to be able to read my mind, I didn't want you to see the wild monkey jumping! Yet perhaps that monkey is trying to hide something, or is afraid to reveal what's beneath the surface.

The past year has been a honeymoon. Everything is so fresh and new, so exciting when seen through the eyes of love. I want to know everything about you. Since you are usually thousands of miles away, I have been getting to know you through your books, your online dharma talks, your life story, your practices of mindful walking and sitting, and through the simplicity of my own breath. When I'm reading your books or listening to dharma talks, certain words or phrases seem to resonate in my heart with an understanding that is beyond my mind. I feel a growing intimacy with you that I cannot explain. It surprises me to realize that I have fallen head over heels in love with a monk!

Becoming a Bell of Mindfulness

June 13

Dear Thay,

It's rainy and unusually cold this afternoon, so I decided to take a nap after lunch. It has been a full retreat, and it feels like a luxury to relax and snuggle under the blankets. I can hear the gentle patter of rain on the roof, and feel a cool breeze drifting in through the window. As my breathing begins to slow down, my body relaxes and transitions into that moment just before sleep. As I slip into that liminal space between waking and dreaming, I have a dream that is so vivid, I'm not sure what's real and what's not.

In the dream, I am sitting in meditation with a long line of monks with clean-shaven heads and long brown robes. We are settled deep in meditation. A bell sounds, and I feel the circular vibration of the bell moving through my body. As the sound continues to dissolve back into silence, I lose a sense of my body, as if I'm dissolving into space. I feel myself slowly becoming the low hum and vibration, as if I am actually becoming the sound of the bell, moving out in ever-widening spirals, into space.

When I wake, I can still feel the vibration of the bell throughout my body. I still hear the unmistakable sound of the bell all around me.

I lie very still, in touch with both the world of my dream and the physical surroundings of my room. I know from dream work that dreams often contain messages from our unconscious, and perhaps even from the universal consciousness that connects us all. As I feel into this vibration, I wonder "What does it mean to become the bell?" You often teach that we can all become "bells of mindfulness" for each other simply by the way we breathe and walk and eat and treat each other. You and your monastics are bells of mindfulness, reminding all of us to slow down, to feel our steps on the earth, to get in touch with both our suffering and joy.

But this dream feels like something else as well. It has an initiatory feel to it, as if I have just been initiated into a new way of being. To be sitting with a long line of monks suggests transmission from a long lineage of ancestral teachers, all the way back to the Buddha. Yet I can also feel a connection to the long lineage of Christian saints and mystics who have preserved the original teachings of the Christ beyond the religion that bears his name. The phrase "blessed to be a blessing" comes to mind, and I am filled with a deep sense of gratitude for the many teachers who have crossed my path—but especially for you, dear Thay, and the love that you embody. Can I be a bell of mindfulness for both the Buddha and the Christ, and fully live into my name "Divine Oneness of the Heart?" Can I somehow give voice to this growing love that wants to overflow from my heart, like the sound of the bell flowing out in ever-widening circles?

Savor: Mindful Eating, Mindful Life

We have to learn ways to eat that preserve the health and well-being of our body, our spirit, and our planet.
Thich Nhat Hanh and Dr. Lilian Cheung, *Savor: Mindful Eating, Mindful Life*

June 15
Dear Thay,
Yesterday, as I made my way to take the bus to Upper Hamlet for your dharma talk, I found myself standing beside a beautiful Asian woman with a welcoming smile. We greeted each other, then started a quiet conversation. I found out that she is the Director of Health Promotion at Harvard, and has co-written a book with you called *Savor: Mindful Eating, Mindful Life*. What an amazing experience and honour that must be, to co-write a book with you.

Later that evening, Dr. Lilian Cheung gave an insightful overview of her research, and the book. Everything Lilian said resonated deeply as an embodied practice I've somehow already absorbed. "You are what you eat" is such a true statement for me. I would also add "You are how you eat." So many people live in a fast food culture that doesn't give them time to truly sit and savour their food, to be grateful for the many hands that have brought it to their table, and to feel how everything they put in their mouth connects them to the precious web of life. Instead, people grab a quick bite while checking email, watching TV, or reading a book. We rarely sit down and just enjoy the simple and sacred act of eating.

Meals here at Plum Village are different. They are silent and slow and peaceful, giving us time to fully enjoy and absorb the energy and nutrition of our food. Mindfully lining up in silence, often in long line-ups, means we also have the opportunity to feel the hunger in our bellies, and to anticipate the abundance of nutritious vegan food lovingly prepared by the monks and nuns. Our dharma family has the wonderful job of cutting and preparing vegetables. It is such a delight to see how the carrot or beet I chopped shows up in our food. Before serving ourselves, we bring our hands together in front of our hearts and bow to the utensils and food, with gratitude for what we will receive. Remembering to "eat simply so others may live," we are careful not to overfill our plates, to take only as much as we will eat. Together with others, I often like to take my food outside, in the Buddha garden. I begin by looking at the plate, and say a silent blessing. I remember your gatha, "Beings all over the Earth are struggling to live. I aspire to practice deeply so that all may have enough to eat." This is a deep prayer of inter-being. With the sun shining above, and the grass growing beneath me, eating outside deepens the connection between myself and the food, the farmers who grew it, and the monks and nuns who have prepared it. I can almost taste the kindness cooked into every morsel. I am reminded that this food contains the very essence of life that keeps us alive. When I eat like this, not only does the food taste more delicious, everything around me becomes more vibrant and real.

After eating, I take a moment to look at my empty plate, grateful that I now have a full belly. Slowly, I take my plate and utensils to line up again in the washing line. I smile at a sign that says "Washing the dishes is like bathing a baby Buddha." As I plunge my hands into the murky water, I try to remember that everything done in mindfulness nourishes the baby Buddha within.

Dr. Cheung's talk on mindful eating included the many benefits of eating a plant-based diet, both for ourselves and our planet. Meat production is such a huge drain on our poor planet. The United Nations report *Livestock's Long Shadow* estimates that raising livestock uses eight percent of our planet's water and aggravates water depletion and pollution. Another report (Johns Hopkins Bloomberg School of Public Health) found that factory farming in the U.S. alone takes a heavy toll on both human health and the health of the environment—and that keeping livestock in these "concentrated animal feeding operations" constitutes inhumane treatment. Meat consumption adds mightily to the production of climate-changing greenhouse gases. The livestock industry produces 18 percent of the world's greenhouse gas emissions, a higher share than the entire transportation sector. Each of these statistics should be reason enough to transition to a kinder, plant-based diet. Together, they create irrefutable evidence that it's time to stop eating meat, or at least cut back on the mass production and cruelty.

Lilian went on to describe the benefits of a plant-based diet. "Vegetarians and vegans tend to weigh less and have lower blood pressure, lower blood cholesterol, and, in turn, a lowered risk of heart disease than people whose diets include animal products; they may also have lower risks of some cancers."[10] How strange that we can read or hear all these facts and still not be convinced. It seems that only when we have direct experience of the harm of a meat-based diet, and the benefits of a plant-based diet, do we choose to transition to making better choices.

When I began the practice of yoga over twenty years ago, I started reading about the yogic principle of "ahimsa," or non-harming. As I began to consider how all of my many actions affected others, I looked into the consumption of meat. *Diet For A Small Planet* by Frances Moore

Lappé showed how we could start to solve world hunger problems by moving towards a plant-based diet. As I helplessly watched pictures of young children starving to death across the world, I decided that I could at least start to make a difference in my own diet.

I didn't quit eating all meat right away. Such deeply ingrained habits can be difficult to change, but slowly I began to eliminate meat from my diet, starting with beef and pork, then chicken, then finally fish and seafood. As I did so, I began to notice a subtle change in the way my body felt, and in my energy. Whereas my body sometimes felt heavy and bloated, I began to notice a feeling of lightness, not necessarily in my weight, but in what yoga calls the "subtle body," the life energy of prana. My mind was affected too. I wasn't as worried or anxious all the time. A space was opening up that was less reactive, and more peaceful.

Lately, as I've listened to you speak about the Four Nutrients and what we are feeding our mind, our body, and our being, I began to wonder if people are consuming the fear and fright, and just the enormous suffering of the animal meat they consume. Could some of society's anxiety and depression be related to the consumption of animals raised and slaughtered under such violent conditions? Even if it's just a small part of the overwhelming fear in society, I'm reminded over and over again "We are what we eat."

The First Blush of a Lotus

Be like the earth. When the rain comes, the earth simply opens up to the rain and soaks it in...A teacher cannot give you the truth. The truth is already in you. A teacher can only offer you the chance to awaken your true self.
Thich Nhat Hanh and Dr. Lilian Cheung, *Savor: Mindful Eating, Mindful Life*

June 16

Dear Thay,

Today before your dharma talk I sat down by the lotus pond, where the sun, already warm on my back, caught tiny droplets of water on the smooth lotus leaves. Once more the sun reflected like thousands of tiny diamonds shimmering in an ocean of mud. Somehow, the lotus pond seems to be a metaphor for what is happening inside me. I think you planned the dates of this bi-annual retreat exactly for that reason. I can imagine the smile of joy it brings you to watch the lotus bloom, both plant and human!

When I first arrived and sat down by the lotus pond, there was only a mass of tangled stems and leaves covering the mystery of what lies beneath. Yet as I have kept returning to sit and breathe quietly, I have felt a sense of aliveness beneath the murky depths. Last week I noticed a few green buds on long stems reaching up out of the depths, towards the sky. The buds were still tightly bound, as if too afraid to open to the full light of the sun. Now they've begun to relax a bit, tinged with the blush of the pink lotus blossoms they will become. Perhaps they are reflecting the tender blush of my heart beginning to open.

I seem to be sinking deeper and deeper into myself and deeper and deeper into you. "Inter-being" now feels like a felt reality instead of just a thought or concept. You encourage us not to take notes during your dharma talks, but simply to allow the words and impressions to penetrate our mind and consciousness like gently falling dharma rain. In today's dharma talk, you talked about inter-being, how body and consciousness interact, like a force field of energy reaching out and interacting with everyone. "We are not only this body, we affect everything. You are in me, and I am in you" you said, as you turned to look at me, reaching out with the full force of your attention. Once more, it was not just the words you said, but a felt experience of "inter-being" in my body.

After the bell at the end of the morning session, I stood very still as you slowly began to leave the meditation hall with your attendants. Other people began to pick up their belongings, but I simply wanted to stay in this peaceful energy of your presence for as long as I could. As you passed by, you turned and gave me a shy smile that reminded me of some of the pictures I've seen of you as a young man. It almost seemed like you were flirting with me in this cosmic game of love we're playing. Perhaps that's the nature of this great Love that flows in and between and through all creation. This Love flirts and plays and winks at us when we accept the invitation to dance.

CHAPTER 12

Vows Engraved Upon My Heart

The Five Mindfulness Trainings are love itself. To love is to understand, protect, and bring well-being to the object of our love...We protect ourselves and each other and we obtain even deeper peace and joy.
Thich Nhat Hanh, *For A Future To Be Possible*

Transmission of the Five Mindfulness Trainings

June 17

Dear Thay,

Today is the Ceremony for the Transmission of the Five Mindfulness Trainings, your version of the precepts the Buddha gave for living more conscious and compassionate lives. With deep insight, you have updated these precepts to be more meaningful and culturally relevant to our times. Yet as you say, they are really just an expression of love.

I already received the transmission, last year in Vancouver, but that was in a university gym, and although my heart was sincere, I'm not sure I really understood what all I was committing to. Now I feel like I have grown both in my understanding of the five trainings, as well as in my relationship with you, my dear teacher. My love for you as a reflection of the "divine indwelling" has blossomed. I want to commit at a deeper level, and experience the transmission here in the quiet serenity of Plum Village.

This morning we got up at 4:30 a.m. to take the bus from New Hamlet to Lower Hamlet, where the 6:30 a.m. Transmission Ceremony will take place. The sun is yet to rise, as the large bus lumbers along narrow twisting roads, and weaves through vineyards and sleepy villages. We practice Bus Meditation, not talking, simply listening to the hum of the bus as background for our thoughts and not quite awake minds.

Arriving at Lower Hamlet, I mindfully walk through the dew-filled grass to the meditation hall, where, taking off my sandals, I feel the coolness of the wood floor beneath my bare feet. Bowing before entering this sacred space, I then pause to look around. Since I am one of the first to arrive, the meditation hall is almost empty, with a silence that beckons me. I walk down a long narrow row of cushions set up in the middle of the hall for those who will soon receive the trainings. I'm not usually a "first-row" kind of person, but this morning it seems important to sit right in the front, both to see and be seen.

With reverence, I bow again, before sitting on the meditation cushion, adjusting my body to sit tall, like the Buddha. I close my eyes and settle into the comfort of my breath. I can sense the room filling up around me with hushed whisperings and quiet steps. The monks and nuns, in ceremonial orange sanghati robes for this special occasion, surround us. It feels like a solid wall of love and support transmitted through many generations of Buddhas and Bodhisattvas. Finally, I feel that shimmering moment of settling into silence, when the group energy of meditation is strong, and we all settle into each other as a living, breathing sangha.

As you invite the large bell, I feel the sound rippling through my body, calling me back to my breath, back to you, back to the Buddha, back to the Living Christ. The pure sound of your clear voice chanting in Vietnamese brings softness to my eyes as the fragrance of incense infuses the whole room with perfume.

In gratitude, we offer this incense throughout space and time to all Buddhas and Bodhisattvas. May it be fragrant as Earth herself, reflecting careful efforts, wholehearted awareness, and the fruit of understanding, slowly ripening...
Incense Offering, *Plum Village Chant*

I feel the teachings ripening in me. As is the custom, we all prostrate and

"Touch the Earth" many times to honour all the Buddhas and ancestral teachers on this path.

The one who bows and the one who is bowed to are both, by nature, empty. Therefore the communication between them is inexpressibly perfect.
Opening Gatha for Touching the Earth, *Plum Village*

Is this how communication works between us my dear teacher, beyond words?
Can I be empty enough to receive your precious teachings?
A monk recites the complete Heart Sutra, ending with the familiar lines:

Gate, gate, paragate, parasamgate, bodhi svaha.

I trust you, dear Thay, to guide me beyond...all the way to the other side.

I take refuge in the Buddha, the one who shows me the way in this life.
I take refuge in the Dharma, the way of understanding and of love.
I take refuge in the Sangha, the community that lives in harmony and awareness.
The Three Refuges, *Plum Village*

I feel the embrace of my teacher, the teachings, and the sangha, like a warm blanket for my soul.

Finally, we receive and commit to each of the Five Mindfulness Trainings, one by one, bowing and touching the earth between each one. What a privilege to be here at Plum Village, to receive the transmission directly from you, dear Thay. I feel the coolness of the wood floor against my forehead as I bow in child's pose (thank goodness for years of yoga practice!). I stretch out my arms, palms up in an attitude of openness and prayer, vowing to live these Five Mindfulness Trainings to the best of my ability.

It feels as if the words are no longer words on a page, but have been imprinted on my heart. I feel the presence of you, my beloved teacher. I trust that you are guiding me in this moment, and in many moments to come. I feel myself relaxing. The nervous young schoolgirl seems to have been replaced by a woman who is secure in herself and her teacher's love.

After the ceremony is over I receive a new Five Mindfulness Trainings certificate from Sister Chân Không, with my dharma name "Divine Oneness of the Heart," reminding me of my deep love for Buddha, for Christ, for Allah, for Krishna, for Shekinah, for Mother Earth, for the Divine that dwells in all. Our dharma family has our pictures taken together, and as I stand beside Sister Chân Không, it almost feels like I'm standing beside you. Shantum Seth, a dharma teacher from India, gives us each a silk bodhi leaf as a symbol, a reminder of awakening on this day. My heart is bursting with gratitude, blessed to be a blessing.

I feel the peace of this moment, and yet my heart is still aflame with the sweet heat of desire for something more. "More what?" I wonder. Will my heart ever be free of this longing, or is this longing and desire the fuel that will keep the fire hot enough to burn through the layers of doubt, and fear, and whatever else keeps me from seeing the true nature of the Love that we all are? "Breathe, my dear," I hear you say.

The Question of My Heart

Dear Thay,

Today, I received an answer to the question of my heart, as if another piece of the puzzle has slipped into place. I was sitting by the bell tower when Quinn, a woman in my dharma family, sat down beside me. We chatted about our retreat experiences, then about the question and answer dharma talk earlier this morning. She's known you for twenty-five years and was a member of the second group ordained to the Order of Inter-being. She explained that when she first met you, you didn't focus as much on how to handle suffering. You taught more about watering the positive seeds of mindfulness, peace and joy. Quinn shared with me that she has always felt happy and blessed. She said it doesn't feel right for her to keep looking for suffering, when she already has so much peace of mind.

That sounds so familiar! I shared that I too feel that way, but I don't always want to admit it. Who wants to admit they don't suffer much when there is so much suffering in the world? Of course I'm not a Buddha yet! I still experience doubt and lack of trust in myself, but that seems to be part of the journey of being human. I trust that will continue to heal in time if I continue to stay mindful. I don't have to force it. There's already enough suffering in the world. I don't have to create more.

As Quinn continued to speak, it felt like my prayers were being answered—that you were speaking through her, assuring me that "yes, just breathe, my dear. Enjoy the peace. Enjoy the happiness. Share it with others, with compassion and love."

Snapshots From a Life

Dear Thay,
I often wish we had met earlier. At the ripe age of eighty-five, it doesn't seem like there can be much time left. It's why the time I do have with you is so precious. Although I receive so much from just being here in retreat with you, there's a part of me that wishes I could have tea or a personal conversation with you. I can't exactly "sit at the feet of the teacher," like in other spiritual traditions. I have to rely on the personal stories of some of your nuns and dharma teachers, and their memories of you. It is so nourishing to hear these simple stories, to have the privilege of seeing snapshots of your life, that of a Zen master outside the public eye.

This afternoon we had Tea Meditation with our dharma sisters and nuns at New Hamlet. It was a tender time of sharing our personal journeys of inner transformation, with lots of laughter and tears. Our suffering and joy truly go hand in hand. Sister Chân Không shared personal stories from your early days in Vietnam and how you continually pushed the boundaries to renew Buddhism to make it relevant—ordaining nuns, removing the formalities, and practicing engaged Buddhism in the midst of war.

Another nun shared a more recent, endearing story. She said she had been trying to get your attention as you walked towards the meditation hall this morning. You were walking faster than you usually do. Finally, you turned to her and said gently "not now," and started walking more quickly towards the lotus pond. As you walked away, she heard you whispering to the first lotus blossom of the season "I'm coming, my dear, I'm coming." I can almost feel that tender and intimate love in my own heart, as the pink blush of the lotus bud opens to the full light of your love.

Plum Village Celebrates Thirty Years

June 20

Dear Thay,

Today we celebrated the thirtieth birthday (or Continuation Day) of Plum Village with a big party, Plum Village style, a testament to your teachings and practices of mindfulness across the globe. There is so much history to celebrate, from the humble beginnings of a rustic farm homestead that became Upper Hamlet, then in time adding Lower Hamlet, and finally New Hamlet. I often wish I could have attended smaller, intimate retreats with you back then. Now they have grown into international retreats of over a thousand people at a time, from all over the world. Still, you certainly realized your dream of creating a healthy, nourishing environment away from the rush of everyday life, where people can learn to live in peace with each other and in harmony with the earth.

We are hosting the celebration at New Hamlet, so there is a flurry of activity to prepare for the arrival of all those from the other hamlets.

There is an exhibit of all the books you have written over the past thirty years, including original copies of your classics *Miracle of Mindfulness* and *Peace Is Every Step*. All the nuns are excited to be preparing for you, our beloved teacher. Their deep love for you shines in their eyes.

Later, that deep love is reflected in your own eyes as you sit in the Buddha garden, watching your New Hamlet Nuns dance and re-enact one of your poems. I see the young Vietnamese boy in you smile excitedly at the next Dragon Dance, as monks transform into a long dragon undulating from side to side with a large fiery head bobbing up and down. After the dances and music, we all enjoy our picnic lunches. With the stone Buddhas in the garden solemnly watching over us, it feels as if we are all sitting around a smiling, living Buddha. I could have sworn I saw one of the stone Buddhas wink! How precious these moments are with you, our teacher so close. I close my eyes to savour the moment, then hear someone announce "Birthday cupcakes!" It's a rare sweet treat at Plum Village. Yes indeed, a sweetness beyond taste flows like honey all through my mind and body. As I look out over the sea of smiling joyful faces, I see bodhisattvas everywhere, spreading like the ocean. It is a deep tribute to your life of compassion and sacred activism.

CHAPTER 13

A Lotus in Full Bloom

The tears you shed yesterday have become rain.
Thich Nhat Hanh, *Calligraphy*

A Single Tear

June 21

Dear Thay,

Today is the last full day of our 21-Day Retreat together. I want to savour every single moment. I practice yoga outside under the bell tower, my body moving to an ancient rhythm as the dawn slowly seeps across the horizon. I sit with the sangha as the quiet power and energy of group meditation permeates my body and my mind. I hear the sound of birds amidst the deepening silence. A monk invites the bell, and once more I feel it vibrating in my every cell.

Finally, it's time for your last dharma talk. I arrive early and sit still in the meditation hall before you arrive. Even though we are still supposed to observe silence, I am aware of the sounds of people rustling around me. The meditation calms my mind and softens my heart. You always say to listen to a dharma talk as if it were gentle rain dissolving into the soil of our consciousness. My body and mind feel especially light and spacious, ready to receive whatever wisdom you want to pour into us.

This morning as the monk's pure voice chants, I am so touched by the beauty of the moment, such gratitude. but also knowing this is my last day, possibly my last time with you, my beloved teacher.

The Dharma body is bringing morning light.
In concentration, our hearts are at peace, a half smile is born upon
our lips.

This is a new day. We vow to go through it in mindfulness.
The sun of wisdom has now risen, shining in every direction.
Noble sangha diligently, bring your mind into meditation.
Namo Shakyamunaye Buddhaya (3 times)
Morning Chant, Plum Village

A single teardrop escapes my eye, runs down my cheek and finally dissolves in the crease of my neck. This single tear seems to contain a lifetime of joy and sorrow. I feel the carefree joy of myself as a young girl running barefoot, and the excitement of a young woman getting ready to leave for college. I see the tears of love in Doug's eyes on our wedding day, and feel the ecstatic joy of hearing our baby's first cry. I feel the all-encompassing joy of being here with you. This joy is intermingled with memories of my grandmother dying on my sixteenth birthday, the hospitalization of our two-year-old son for a brain hemorrhage, and the grief of watching the light in my mother's eyes slowly fade as she took her last, laboured breath.

Can you feel my tears Thay? It feels like this tear is not mine alone but contains the joy and sorrow of my parents and grandparents, my children and grandchildren not yet born. It is a tear that contains the hopes and dreams of all of humanity, as well as the atrocities of war and the dying of our planet. It seems like inter-being has become a felt reality through this single tear.

I call you Beloved in my heart. This morning you talked about the right and left hand as one. Although they appear separate, they work and interact as one. You turned and said "Lover and Beloved are one," looking at me as if you could see the inner transformation that is slowly taking place. I know that part of this transformation is my relationship with you and all the confusing feelings it engenders. So slowly, the lover and Beloved are becoming one. Yet the Beloved is not really Thay, and the lover is not really me. In the end, lover and Beloved dissolve into Love.

At the end of your dharma talk you invited us to your private "Sitting Still" hut to admire the wide expansive view of the whole valley you have during meditation. One of the nuns mentioned that it is quite a rare event for you to invite everyone to your personal meditation hut. After twenty-one days of basking in your presence, it feels like an invitation to something deeper, something unexpected. My heart skips a beat.

The meditation hall has now erupted with the bustle of moving chairs and putting away cushions. I listen to this outside noise from the inner stillness of my heart. I don't want to come out of silence yet. I want to savour these last few moments of the retreat. Slowly, I make my way towards the doors, my eyes searching the rows and rows of shoes for my brown sandals amidst all the other brown sandals. Where did I put my shoes today? My mind is too spacious to remember such minute details. Then, my body brings me back to reality as the pressure in my bladder makes me regret that second cup of tea this morning. After finally spotting my shoes, I make my way over to the long lines that inevitably form at the women's washrooms.

A Visit to Thay's Hut

Earth's crammed with heaven, and every common bush alive with God, But only he who sees takes off his shoes.
Elizabeth Barrett Browning, *Aurora Leigh*

After leaving the restroom, I slowly follow the stream of people towards your Sitting Still Hut in the monastic area that is usually off limits. I walk the well-worn path like I am walking in your footprints. The trees gracefully bow inwards as we descend the steps towards the outer deck, with its stunning view of the tree-lined valley. As I step onto the wooden deck, I notice you sitting to the right, surrounded by a small group of students. I didn't expect to see you here, and it takes me by surprise. Our eyes meet briefly and I feel a small flutter of nervous excitement. Forgetting all my manners, not thinking to bow or to take off my shoes before walking to the front part of the deck, my eyes take in the sweeping view of the valley, with the rolling hills and Catholic monastery in the distance. I feel your eyes watching me. I've heard you say "Looking at a disciple's way of walking, of smiling, of greeting and of being, I can see whether my teaching has been fruitful or not." So I am aware of my every move, my every breath.

I hear the words from the bible of my childhood imprinted on my mind, "Take off your shoes. You are standing on holy ground." I remove my sandals, and enjoy the cool roughness of the wood against my bare feet. I'm not Moses. I see no burning bushes. I simply feel the holiness of this moment, the sacred energy of my teacher's intimate living space.

People line up around the living quarters of your humble hut. Although we are not allowed inside, we are invited along the outer deck, peeking in windows that reveal the intimate living space of our teacher. It is like a walking dharma talk, revealing the profound simplicity and depth of a Zen Buddhist monk's life. I gaze at the desk where you do your writing and calligraphy, and at the stack of meditation cushions stacked neatly in the corner. On the wall I see the picture of you as a sixteen-year-old novice, your eyes reflecting the pure love in your heart and the vision you already have for the future. The small kitchen table is set with a simple orchid and a small teapot ready for you to enjoy a cup of tea. When I spot your little bed in the back corner, I feel as if I am being invited to remove the final layers of armouring around my heart. It is too much for me right now. I wonder, what am I afraid of? Is there still a part of me in shadow that I need to bring into your light, to allow myself to be fully seen and known? Will I have the chance to be in your beloved presence again?

I circle behind the hut, to come back to where you are still sitting. The deck is now filled with people. I find a place on the slope just above your hut, with a clear view framed by the graceful arch of the trees. I feel like Zacchaeus, the tax collector in the Bible, sitting in a tree, watching Jesus. Is there a part of me that still feels unworthy? Every so often you look up at me, and there is the familiar feeling of your all-encompassing love. I also feel the sweet ache of knowing this might be the last time I see you.

It's a bittersweet moment of both joy and sorrow. I feel the tender space in my heart, the memory of the single tear rolling down my cheek; one tear drop containing all my love, all my sadness, all my longing. I remember your words from your earlier dharma talk: "Thay is non-local. I am here, and I am everywhere. I am you and you are me. I am with you always."

One last time, I ask you silently in my mind if I can take your picture, and you turn and gaze directly at me, with the pure love of that young sixteen-year-old monk. It is the most intimate picture, as if you are looking directly in my eyes again, perfectly capturing the feeling and sanctity of this moment. I can allow myself to be fully seen, after all.

A guitar is playing, and Joe Reilly is singing a tender song about love, the words expressing exactly what I want to say. So many of us feel this deep love and devotion. The next song is "Buddha Breathes," and I quietly add my voice, singing softly beneath the canopy of sky and trees.

Finally, you stand up and we follow you on a long walk to the heart of the Buddha Forest. Once more, I take off my shoes. I feel like I am still walking on holy ground, "kissing the earth" with my bare feet. Perhaps all ground is holy when we take time to notice. This ground is wet and slippery in places, and I feel the mud between my toes. The wind has picked up and it feels like all of us will soon be scattered like falling leaves. Change and expectation are in the air.

Afterwards, I eat lunch quietly, sitting by the bell tower above your hut, savouring this last moment of being close to you. Even though I know you are always with me, there is something special about being in your physical presence. I wonder, will I see you again?

When I get back to New Hamlet, I walk silently towards the lotus pond. It has blossomed, come alive in the last few days—a sea of vibrant pink lotus blossoms rising up out of the mucky depths below. I'm drawn to one single lotus flower adorned with several large green leaves. It seems to be smiling just for me. A single drop of water sits like a diamond on the smooth surface of the leaf. I watch it sparkle in the light until it finally evaporates in the afternoon sun.

My Mother Smiles at Me

June 22

Dear Thay,

It's time to travel back to my home in Canada today. Stuffing the last few items into my oversized suitcase, I reach up and carefully place my mother's Tilley hat on my head. I found this hat when I was going through her things after she died, carefully tucked away in its original packaging. The hat had never been used. I smile at the image of the old tattered sunbonnet she used to wear, when she had this sturdy hat tucked away in a drawer. I vowed to wear this hat as a way to take her with me, somehow, wherever I traveled. She has traveled here to France with me, and will travel to Nepal and India this fall. The gift of her small inheritance has allowed me to travel and see the world. In return, I walk for her.

Pausing at the door of the small room where I have slept for the past twenty-one days, I chuckle to myself as I look at the sign on the door: "Bodhi." I have received many small glimpses of enlightenment here, but no one moment can I point to and say "That's it!" You always say that enlightenment is made of many smaller moments. I will continue to practice and notice those small moments.

I lug my suitcase down the creaky steps of the old farmhouse. It's not easy to be quiet here! Slowly, I begin the familiar walk between the farmhouse and New Hamlet, my breath easily in sync with each step. Without even thinking about it, this way of walking and breathing and being has become a habit. All my senses are awake, enjoying the kaleidoscope of sights and sounds of life all around me.

As I gaze out over the fields, I notice a single sunflower in the middle of one field, and it brings another tender tear to my eye, reminding me once more of my dear mother. Last year at this time she was in the last few weeks of her life. Later, when choosing flowers for her service of remembrance, the florist kept showing me all kinds of fancy flower arrangements. Nothing seemed right, until I noticed some simple sunflowers sitting in the corner of the shop. I knew that's what my mother would choose. So now, as I see this lone sunflower, I see my mother smiling at me. Her Tilley hat on my head feels like the gentle weight of her loving hand, assuring me she's still here.

Dear Thay, you teach that when we breathe and walk mindfully and solidly on the earth, we are walking for our parents and grandparents and children. My mother was caught in very rigid beliefs about God and religion, and I was never able to share with her my feelings about the oneness underlying all religions. She suffered greatly because of her beliefs. As I walk, I know that I have somehow helped transform both our suffering. I walk for her. And I am walking for my children, and their children, while the sunflower quietly smiles her beautiful smile. Perhaps one day I will come back to Plum Village when the fields are full of sunflowers, smiling with the kind of golden joy that cannot be contained in just one flower, one body, one religion.

Photograph by Vickie MacArthur

CHAPTER 14

New Insights, New Questions

Please look into the river of your own life and see the many streams that have entered it, that nourish and support you.
Thich Nhat Hanh, *Cultivating the Mind of Love*

Beloved Communities

July 16

Dear Thay,

Our family has travelled to Samish Island, off the coast of Washington state, for our church's annual summer family camp. Like Plum Village, Samish Island is a sacred place where our Christian community gathers to live in harmony with God and the earth. Our sons, Brendan and Andrew, have been loved and nurtured in this safe and inclusive community. Doug and I have many dear spiritual friends here, and a lifetime of memories.

Still, although I love this community, camps and retreats here are loud, bustling with activity and conversation. There is a felt sense of love and aliveness, but Silence often sits alone in the corner waiting for people to "be still, and notice." The dining room is especially loud and boisterous at meal times. Although a blessing is said before the meal, there is no bell to invite people to be quiet and come back to this moment of really tasting our food, while gazing out the windows at the ocean and the occasional blue heron gracefully drifting by. My newly awakened heart yearns for silence and solitude. I often escape the noise and chatter to wander down by the oyster beds close to the ocean, or walk the winding paths of the Blue Heron sanctuary.

I invite you to walk these holy grounds with me.

We walk into the forest, and veering off on a little path, encounter a small wooden fenced area, around a tombstone. "Harry Samish. Died June 6, 1899, Age Unknown," the stone says. There is an offering of shells and feathers, so someone is honoring his memory and this space. I wonder about the original inhabitants here, and offer a prayer of gratitude to the Coast Salish people for their deep and abiding connection to this land. On this beautiful sunny day, surrounded by trees, their branches gracefully swaying in welcome, I accept their invitation to simply sit and enjoy the peaceful aliveness of the forest. Yet a part of me is still longing for more. I want to fall in love with Mother Earth, and love Her in the same way that you do, to sense her heartbeat in mine, to feel our "inter-being," our Oneness.

I have invited you to share in my Christian community here, to feel the love of this beloved community that has nurtured the seeds of faith in me my whole life. Could you see those seeds in my heart when you first looked in my eyes? I continue to talk to you, sharing moments of quiet wonder as we look at the sky, or contemplating our shared history in the forest—you and I, Buddhist and Christian, Plum Village and Community of Christ, Harry Samish, this island, these people, the very ground we sit on. I wonder, can you still read my thoughts and feel my love over this physical distance? Do you miss me like I miss you?

I look for answers. Perhaps if I listen deep enough, I will hear you in the wind in the trees, or the waves on the shore. "Be patient, breathe my dear," I hear you say. Yet my mind still seems distracted, full of thoughts of you. I'm not sure how to do this, how this relationship with you works beyond Plum Village. Perhaps it's only a matter of time and I just need to practice and be patient. I have so many questions and doubts when I am away from you. Somehow in your presence they all seem to dissolve, or not matter quite as much. I wish I could sit with you, like a devoted disciple at the master's feet, aware of your every word and breath. But maybe it's not really a matter of physical proximity, but rather a merging of our hearts and consciousness on a deeper level. In one of your old dharma talks, you said "Transmission happens every day in a very simple way. If the teacher/student relationship is good, then that transmission is realised in every moment of our daily life. You don't feel far away from your teacher. You feel that he is, she is, always with you because the teacher outside has become the teacher inside." 11   Yes, when I take time to listen inwards, you are there, whether I'm here at Samish Island, at home in Lethbridge, or in your physical presence at Plum Village. You're only a breath away. I can dip into the river of your love wherever I am.

Because of the Mud, The Lotus Can Bloom

A lotus can never grow without mud. We cannot plant a lotus in a bowl of marbles. So just as the mud plays a very vital role in bringing out the lotus, suffering plays a vital role in bringing out understanding and compassion..
Thich Nhat Hanh, *Awakening of the Heart*

July 21
Dear Thay,
In Vancouver, when I thought I had gotten up on stage to ask you the "question of my heart," time ran out. Instead of asking a question, everything dissolved in that timeless moment you held me in your gaze. Later, when I traveled to Plum Village, I thought about getting up again to ask a question, but sensing you could read my mind, I felt too nervous. The questions keep coming up, and they seem to be part of the spiritual journey. So I keep asking questions, not satisfied with easy answers or even the answers of my own dear teacher.

What do I really know for certain? Do I really know what I think I know, or have I just taken on the beliefs and opinions of others? You have a calligraphy that says "Are you sure?" No, I'm not sure at all, but I'm willing to sit and breathe in this place of not knowing. Will you sit with me here and listen to my story, dear Thay?

Hospital Ward Wisdom: Andrew's Story

My life is not untouched by the everyday pain and suffering that is part of living and loving in this journey called life. Yet our experience of pain and suffering is unique to each and every one of us, depending on our history, our family, our culture, our thoughts, our beliefs, and many other endless variables.

August 18, 1999 is a date embedded in my memory forever. That was the day the movers were scheduled to arrive at our Vancouver home to pack, so we could move to Toronto. Doug was all set to start classes at York University, to complete a master's program in theatre. Little did we know it would be the beginning of a very stressful time for our family. This experience would touch us so deeply, our lives would never be the same.

At 6:30 a.m. that day, as I was doing last-minute packing, Doug came running out of our bedroom, holding our two-year-old Andrew, limp in his arms. "There's something terribly wrong with Andrew. Call 911!" I had never heard Doug use this voice before. Andrew's tiny right hand was clenching and unclenching convulsively. His right eye twitched uncontrollably, while his breath came in stuttering gasps. What could possibly be wrong with our precious little boy? He had gone to bed peacefully the night before, after we'd talked about the great adventure of moving east and being closer to Grandma and Grandpa Mac.

With shaky fingers, I pressed 911. "Police, fire or ambulance?" the voice on the other end of the phone asked. "Ambulance," I said in a trembling voice that did not seem like my own. I looked frantically at Doug, and gave what little details I knew to the operator.

"Mommy, what's wrong with Andrew?" The big brown eyes of Brendan, our six-year-old, were wide with fright. Brendan stood in a corner of the living room, looking lost and confused in his Pokemon pajamas. Suddenly remembering that we had another son who also needed my attention, I took a deep breath and took him in my arms. I explained that we weren't sure what was wrong with Andrew, but that help was on its way. I suggested that he help by watching out the window to let us know when the ambulance got to our house.

After what seemed like forever, the ambulance finally pulled up, lights flashing. Surrounded by huge stacks of moving boxes, the paramedics examined our little boy. Andrew had stopped twitching by this time. "Looks like he's just had a petit mal seizure," the paramedic said matter-of-factly. "But you should probably get him checked out." Yes indeed, I thought. Kids don't have seizures for no reason! Since there didn't seem to be any immediate danger, they suggested we could drive him ourselves to BC Children's Hospital in Vancouver, where hopefully pediatric specialists could determine what was wrong.

It was now almost 7:30. The movers were due at 8. Sitting on the couch, our two boys between us, feeling numb, unable to think straight, Doug and I had no idea what to do. I called Lanette and explained what had happened. Without a moment's hesitation, Lanette rushed over and took charge. She would drive Andrew and me to the hospital, while Doug stayed back to deal with the movers.

When we arrived at the emergency department, Andrew had another round of seizures. As the triage nurse asked me questions, I mentioned that my mom had been visiting to help with the move and had developed a severe case of shingles. As soon as I said that the nurse picked up the phone. "Isolation room needed," she said calmly. With lightning speed we were whisked into a sterile examining room.

The long day continued. Andrew was examined by a steady stream of doctors that ended, finally, with a neurologist accompanied by his intern. Andrew continued to have seizures intermittently through the day, but without a diagnosis, the doctors did not want to give him any medication.

As I waited, I held Andrew in the patchwork quilt he'd been given as a baby. Robert Munsch's *Love You Forever* was one of Andrew's favorite bedtime stories. "Sing me the song, Mommy," Andrew would always say. In a trembling voice I sang it now, tears streaming down my face, into the puppy dog faces of Andrew's favorite blanket. "I'll love you forever, I'll like you for always. As long as I'm living, my baby you'll be."[12]

I tried to imagine a future of Andrew growing up into a young man, with a family of his own, and smiled at Munch's image of a mother driving through dark streets in an old battered station wagon, with a ladder strapped onto the roof, ready to sneak into her grown-up son's house and sing him this song.

Finally, an EEG confirmed seizure activity in the brain, and Andrew was started on the first of many anti-convulsive medications. Doug arrived late in the afternoon, looking drained and tired, his eyes searching mine for answers I did not yet have. The movers had emptied our house. Everything we owned was packed onto a truck headed for Toronto. We were officially homeless, stuck between the life we had planned and the uncertainty of a new life we could not yet name.

Andrew was placed in the neurology ward, and just as we were getting settled, our good friend and minister, Brian Gibson, arrived. We found a small hospital chapel, where we could have some peace and quiet after our long grueling day. As Brian gently laid his hands on Andrew's head and gave a heartfelt prayer for healing and strength, I felt the adrenaline that had kept me going drain away into bone-deep fatigue.

Leaving the hospital chapel, I noticed a prayer book where family and loved ones could write a thought, a prayer, or whatever they needed to express. There were so many names, each one with their own story. I wondered about each name. Where were they now? Did God hear these prayers? Why were some children healed and others not? I had no answers. Instead, I said a silent prayer for them all as I added Andrew's name to the list.

During the next few days, Andrew underwent all kinds of tests and scans to determine the reason for the seizures. Although they could not confirm for sure, the doctors suspected that a malformed blood vessel on the left side of Andrew's brain had bled, causing partial seizures on the right side of his body. In the meantime, the doctors tried a cocktail of powerful anti-convulsive medications to try to get the seizures under control.

Although it was an extremely challenging time, we were surrounded by the love and support of a network of caring church friends and family. It is truly amazing how people take time out of their own busy lives to come together in the face of trying circumstances. Since we had no home to return to, Lanette and Phil opened their home to us and became Brendan's surrogate parents when we were at the hospital with Andrew. We were truly embraced and surrounded. The care and support of our community sustained us through this traumatic time.

Andrew's seizures proved intractable. The doctors continued to try one powerful drug after another. A lot of these were given intravenously, and it was difficult to watch our active two-year-old succumb to the initial side-effects of these potent drugs. He became clumsy and unbalanced, almost like he was learning to walk again. Wearing a helmet on his head in case he fell, he needed constant supervision and attention. I pretty well lived at the hospital during this time.

Near the beginning of September, when Andrew seemed to be improving, Doug and Brendan finally flew out to Toronto. Both of them needed to start school at our new home there. It was hard to split our family up at such a difficult time, and good-byes were tearful.

The days stretched into weeks, and the weeks to a month as I began to settle into the routine of hospital life. Occasionally, I would get the chance to slip up onto the hospital roof and terrace garden by myself. Often, a Muslim man was there with his prayer mat unfolded, his body and lips moving in an ancient rhythm of prayer. The roof top became our temple and mosque, a sacred space to retreat to for prayers and meditation. There, under sunny Vancouver skies, I would lay out my yoga mat, facing towards English Bay and the North shore mountains, and let my body flow through the familiar postures of my yoga sun salutations as my own form of prayer. Occasionally, a few stray tears would come unexpectedly, and I would rest back in child's pose. Arms outstretched, forehead on the ground, I would allow my mind and body to release the worry and fear that often gripped me. As the warm breeze caressed my skin, I would feel a sense of timelessness, a kind of acceptance that everything was going to be okay no matter what the future held. Perhaps I was learning the deeper lessons of yoga as I learned to accept "what is" instead of what I thought "should be."

Something was beginning to shift in me. Instead of being consumed by my worry and concern for Andrew, I was blessed with a sense of calm and reassurance. This allowed me to begin to open my eyes to the experiences of all the other children and their families on the neurology ward at B.C. Children's Hospital. As we shared our stories, I felt other families' pain and shared their hope, deeply touched by the courage and compassion I saw all around me. Many of these stories were heartbreaking. Marina-Lina, a fifteen-month-old Hispanic girl, had been having unexplained seizures for eight months. Her mother's tireless love showed in every heartfelt touch and action. We watched baby Cody, a tiny newborn, his bandaged head swelling from recent brain surgery, looking so lost and alone in the large metal crib. His teenage mother, unsure of how to cope with this needy baby, had abandoned him, so the nurses would often bring this tiny bundle into the nurses' station to care for him there. One-year-old Terence had just been diagnosed with an inoperable brain tumour. His Vietnamese father wandered the halls aimlessly, looking for someone he could share his story with. I would often sit with him, and simply listen to his story over and over again as his grief spilled out all around us. Something about listening to this father's deep grief interwoven with his pure love allowed the crack in my own heart to stretch wider without breaking. Telling our stories to each other, we were able to find understanding, and through this experience of deep listening, find the courage to face our own individual battles. The hospital ward was becoming a kind of sangha that held our collective pain and suffering.

I found myself adding each child's name to my prayers as I prayed for Andrew. Yet with these prayers came the same old questions. Why is one child healed, and not another? Who decides? What exactly is prayer? I'm still not sure what the answer to these questions is, but I do know that my life was transformed by this hospital ward wisdom. I had lived such a comfortable and insulated life, completely unaware of the very real suffering that some families live with on a daily basis. Through this experience, I was becoming more open and sensitive to the needs of people around me. I was filled with more compassion, more love, and a greater appreciation for the gift of life itself.

Now, all these years later, I look back on that time, and wonder. In his song "Anthem," Canadian singer-songwriter Leonard Cohen says "There is a crack, a crack in everything. That's how the light gets in."[13] Perhaps the crack that widened in my heart in the hospital allowed me to be open to the light of Thay's love in the depths of grief after losing my mother.

One week after Doug and Brendan left for Toronto, Andrew's seizures worsened. He would have clusters of seizures, one after another. The neurologist suggested that surgery might be the only way to stop them. Tearfully, I called Doug in Toronto. Somehow, he was able to catch a flight across the country that same night. Once more our family was split up, only this time it was Brendan all by himself with Grandma and Grandpa MacArthur, in a new city, starting Grade 1 in a new school. My heart was breaking for both my babies!

The day after Doug arrived, we had a consultation with the neurosurgeon. He suggested that since the anti-convulsive meds didn't seem to be working, surgery might be the only option to try and clean up the scarring from the bleed. With surgery came the risk that Andrew could lose some of the motor function on the right side of his body. It was a heart-wrenching decision, filled with a lot of soul-searching and prayers.

When we got back to Andrew's room that night we received devastating news about a close family friend and minister. Uncle Alf had fallen down the basement steps and sustained a severe head injury. He was lying in a coma only a few blocks away, at Vancouver General Hospital. We were not related by blood, but Alf was the kind of man that everyone called "uncle" because of his kind and generous nature, especially for children. Filled with a deep sadness, we added another name to our prayer list.

Early the next morning, as I walked with Andrew in his stroller around the hospital grounds, my thoughts turned to Uncle Alf, and I began to say a silent prayer for him. Sometimes in the passage between birth and death, the veils between dimensions are especially thin, and this was one of those moments. I felt what I can only describe as Alf's presence, reassuring me that Andrew was going to be all right and that he didn't need the surgery. Later, when I got back to Andrew's room, I received the news that Uncle Alf had passed away around the time that Andrew and I had taken our stroll. Life is mystery. Somehow I know these incidents are all connected. They "inter-are." I believe that in some unexplainable way, Uncle Alf played a part in Andrew's healing.

Miraculously, in the next few days, Andrew's seizures lessened, and our active two-year-old returned. And finally, although his seizures weren't completely under control, he was released from hospital. The date was September 20, over a month since his first seizure. We'd lived a lifetime in that month. Two days later we all flew to Toronto for a joyful reunion with Brendan, and Doug's parents. Home at last! It had been a long journey of both suffering and joy. Out of the mud, a lotus has started to bloom.

A Letter I Actually Send

September 29, 2012

Dear Thay,

It seems like only yesterday I was enjoying the sunshine and gentle spring breezes with you at Plum village during the 21-Day Retreat. Now, the unusually hot summer we had here in Canada is giving way to the cool crispness of autumn.

Yesterday I took another Lazy Day. What a respite from the busyness of life, just time to relax and enjoy the changing colours of fall. I walked in the coulees—a French-Canadian word for flowing—down by the river bottom close to where I live. I flowed along with the river and my breath. As usual, I invited you to walk with me. I also invited the Buddha, the Christ, and my mother. We're quite the crowd when we all walk together! Emma scampers along beside us, following her own path of succulent scents and smells, wagging her tail in the joy of the moment. As we walked, the melodious song of the birds, the flutter and crunch of the fall leaves, and the deep stillness of the forest brought back memories of Plum Village. It's like your presence is imprinted both inside, and all around me.

When I got home, I reread my journal entries from the retreat and felt a strong urge to print and actually send them to you. One click of my keyboard, and I sent off my letter, along with my memories of the 21-Day Retreat. I hope somehow these memories will reach you and bring a smile to your face and a lightness to your heart, perhaps just in time for your upcoming birthday in October. I will be traveling in Nepal and India then, with a charity I support called World Accord.[14] We will meet with local partners and visit remote villages to discover new ways of helping those areas with sustainable development. The work brings to mind some of what you organized in Vietnam in the 1960s, with the School of Youth and Social Service, establishing schools and health clinics. We will also visit some of the holy temples and shrines, both Buddhist and Hindu. It will be a deep experience, to think about walking where the Buddha walked and to be in the midst of Buddhist culture and art. I know that you will walk with me, and I will walk for you in this holy place.

With love and devotion, Vickie
Divine Oneness of the Heart

PART 4

Fanning the Flame

*The Beloved ignites the spark that becomes this fire because
He wants us to come Home, to make the greatest journey,
the soul's journey back to God.*
Llewellyn Vaughan-Lee, *Love is a Fire*

CHAPTER 15

The Path of Love and Devotion

*When we ask a guru to be present, we are asking that this being's
inner state of clarity, love and subtle Awareness come alive in us.
We are opening ourselves to the light inside us.*
Sally Kempton, *Meditation for the Love of It*

The Nature of the Teacher/Disciple Relationship

January, 2013

Dear Thay,

Just one look from you ignited this holy flame of love and longing in my heart. What exactly is the nature of the relationship between spiritual teacher and disciple? This has become the question of my heart that consumes my every waking thought, and even my dreams. Before receiving your mesmerizing gaze of love, I would occasionally read about other people's relationship with their guru or teacher, and be judgmental, or skeptical about their stories. I would question the depth of emotional love they expressed. When I read *Autobiography of a Yogi*, I had absolutely no frame of reference for the seemingly mystical relationship between Yogananda and his guru, Sri Yukteswar. While I have had many wise and wonderful yoga and meditation teachers over the years, the feelings I had for them were more about loving kindness and gratitude. I read Rumi's poetry about his mad passionate relationship with Shams, and again it was just words, a story of someone else's experience. I had no first-hand experience of that kind of teacher. I could not understand that connection in my mind, let alone feel it in my heart.

Then I met you and gazed into the ever-reflecting mirror of your loving eyes. Everything changed in that one timeless moment. Now I know! I know it for myself! There is no need to rely on the words of others. No matter what other people may think or say, I cannot deny my own experience. Spiritual teacher Osho says "In the presence, some day, sitting silently, not knowing, not trying, not desiring, it happens. It happens like a flash of light, and your whole life is transformed."[15] That's key to this experience. I did not knowingly seek this relationship with you. There was no conscious desire to "meet my guru." I went with a raw and grieving heart, having just lost my mother to cancer. Then wham! Out of the blue, the power of your consciousness pulled me out of the crowd, catapulting me onto the stage with you to receive an experience of love that is beyond the rational, planning mind.

The nature of these kinds of mystical experiences is that they never come when we are filled with expectation or clinging to preconceived ideas. They surprise us in such unusual and delightful ways. They let us peek into how an enlightened soul moves through life, and how life moves through them. That sacred moment with you had a sensual quality, like the light feathery touch of butterfly wings on my heart. call it a "shakti kiss," the energy of creation, the touch of Spirit on my skin, and it has opened an invisible thread of communion between our hearts. Even though we are miles apart, I can feel your presence energetically, in my heart. You are present in my every breath, my every step, my every thought, my every action. I am caught in daydreams of you. You are like my secret imaginary friend and teacher. I talk to you in my mind, much the same way I talk to God, asking questions, telling you the secrets of my heart.

Like any new love, I wanted to find out all I could about my new lover. Since I couldn't come and live at Plum Village, I learned all I could through reading your books. I began to have a weekly "date night" with you, watching your online dharma talks. Although I've read other spiritual books, and watched other online talks, this experience was different. It seemed like some kind of spiritual transmission line had been opened between us. It wasn't just the meaning of the words I understood in my mind, it was the lived experience in my body.

Still, this has been a lonely path. Society doesn't acknowledge these kinds of experiences. Most people don't understand this kind of mystical heart connection. If people knew the true depth of my feelings for you, they would think I've gone completely crazy. Even I sometimes wonder. Are there other spiritual seekers who have this kind of mystical heart connection with their teacher? The answer is a resounding Yes! As I have begun my quest to understand the relationship between spiritual teachers and their students, between guru and disciple, I have discovered that I am not the only one consumed by this kind of spiritual love. I've been reading everything I can get my hands on, from Hindu Gurus to Christian Saints, from Sufi Sheikhs to Buddhist masters, from ancient stories to modern-day mystics.

I've begun to understand that one of the ways that spiritual masters relate to their students is through the path of bhakti, or love and devotion. I've discovered that I'm not really alone on this path at all. If anything, I'm in good company. Although Bhakti is rooted in the yogic tradition, the path of love and devotion to the One is present in all spiritual traditions, and called by many different names. Bhakti yoga is sometimes described as Guru Kripa, meaning "the grace of the guru." Although it is usually rooted in one spiritual tradition, the Love it points to takes us beyond these artificial religious boundaries.

The path of bhakti yoga perfectly encompasses my inter-spiritual heart. This love cannot be contained in just one spiritual tradition. Ram Dass calls it a "path or merging with the One through your relationship to an enlightened being." You are that enlightened teacher for me. Bhakti is a path that begins with the emotion of human love, then takes you far beyond. Sally Kempton describes it as a dance between the "devotional emotional part that loves the melting sweetness of an open heart," and the "objective knower that holds all experience in spacious awareness."[16] The essence of Bhakti yoga can take us from dualism to non-dualism, through the great heart of a realized being like yourself.

As my love for you keeps growing, I keep touching that love through you. You are like a mirror that shows me my own beauty, my own face before I was born. I'm beginning to realize your love doesn't have a boundary. Your love includes me. It includes you. It includes everyone and everything. Through your teachings and your practices, and my own open heart, I feel myself merging into your great heart of Love for all beings, and love for Mother Earth

I think Jesus was expressing the path of bhakti when he said "Thou shalt love the Lord thy God with all thy heart, and with all thy soul, and with all thy mind." We need to find a way to love God with our whole being.

Sadly, many people have missed the true depth and meaning of this invitation, understanding it only in the duality of their mind, and not allowing its true force to sink into their body and heart. This is understandable, since God as a concept is difficult to understand. Many of us need a human form we can fall in love with. It's why Christ took on human form, not as a sacrificial lamb, but as a living, breathing example of self-emptying love. Love incarnate. That incarnational love infused his disciples and followers. Praying the prayer of St. Francis, I keep praying to become an instrument of peace, a vessel of love that can spill love out in the same kind of lavish extravagance as Mary Magdalene and her perfume.

Many spiritual teachers stress the practice of true devotion as the easiest path to God-realization. Still, there's a lot to give up in the process, yet on this path, the emptying and renunciation of the disciple happen naturally. Nothing needs to be suppressed. Everything is welcome, including the intensification of love and longing for God, until we finally merge with and remember the Love we already are. This is not the love of personality. It is not the love of romance. It is not a needy kind of love. It is conscious unconditional love.

Through this mystical love, I'm beginning to understand at a visceral level the great love affair between Rumi and Shams, as well as other sufi poets like Hafiz and Kabir. I continue to stay up late enthralled by stories about Neem Karoli Baba and the love he awoke in Ram Dass, Jai Uttal, Krishna Das, and many other well-known teachers in that tradition.

Studying the Christian mystics with Mirabai Starr, I fell in love with Teresa of Avila and St. John of the Cross. I have read modern Christian mystics Richard Rohr and Cynthia Bourgeault, who are quietly transforming the face of Christianity, recovering the contemplative practices of the desert fathers and mothers, and letting go of the dogma of traditional Christian doctrine. I have visited Yashodhara Ashram near Nelson, B.C. and discovered the mystical love affair between Swami Sivananda Radha and her Guru, Swami Sivananda. I have felt the love that Deva Premal and Miten have for Osho, through their music and chants. I read Andrew Harvey's passionate writing about everything from Rumi, to the Christ and the reclaiming of the Divine Feminine, from his devastating break-up with Mother Meera, to finally finding the love beyond religion in Father Bede Griffiths at Shantivanam, a Hindu Christian Ashram. I have studied Heart Yoga with both Andrew and Karuna, and found the sacred marriage of yoga and mysticism that had been missing for me. I have written through my intimate feelings and discovered the answers to my own questions through Mark Matousek's "Writing to Awaken," and listened to stories of his enduring relationship with Mother Meera. I have read Irina Tweedie's *Daughter of Fire*, and through her life story connected to the writings of Llewellyn Vaughn Lee, and the Sufi path of cultivating the union of lover and Beloved for the kind of love we need to re-imagine a new way of relating to each other and to our beloved planet. It feels like random pieces of a puzzle coming together. And yet, I can't quite see the full picture.

Neem Karoli Baba and Ram Dass

To gaze into the eyes of such beings or to hear of their lives resonates within each of us in a place where we know. These eyes are windows on eternity, a mirror of the Self that we share.
Ram Dass, *Be Love Now*

Dear Thay,

Watching an interview on YouTube between you and Ram Dass, I found myself wondering if you could read his mind, like his own teacher, Maharaj-ji, could. Ram Dass was known as a devotee of Eastern religion based in Maharaj-ji's own Hindu religion, yet he also had an inter-spiritual heart that embraced Buddhism, Sufism and Jewish mystical studies.

In 1967, Ram Dass traveled to India, where he met Neem Karoli Baba, the Hindu spiritual teacher known as Maharaj-ji, who would become his spiritual guru. It was Maharaj-ji who gave him his spiritual name, Ram Dass, meaning servant of God. Ram Dass stayed in India with his guru for an extended time, then was blessed by Maharaj-ji to go and share the teachings in North America. Ram Dass went on to write many books, including the classic *Be Here Now*, becoming a much-loved and revered teacher in his own right. Still, it's his personal story and relationship with his guru that I'm most attracted to.

Like me, Ram Dass met Maharaj-ji just after his mother died of cancer. During their first encounter, Maharaj-ji told Ram Dass what he'd been thinking about his mother the previous night. This literally blew Ram's mind, and he felt like "something in me shattered, and I just began to sob." In that moment, Ram Dass knew that this teacher "knew." So began Ram's life-long spiritual love affair with Neem Karoli Baba.

Ram Dass describes the experience of darshan, or "the gaze of the guru" like looking into the eyes of the Buddha: "The universe disappears. Only his eyes exist. A flow of love, wisdom, consciousness passes between you...You feel as if you were naked before his glance. He sees through you, he knows all – past, present, future. He does not judge, but simply acknowledges how it all is."[17] Ram Dass's description of "the gaze of the guru" so perfectly mirrors my own experience with you. I too feel like I have looked into the eyes of a living Buddha. However, while there is a universality to this timeless gaze of Divine Love, I've learned that each person receives it according to their capacity and life experiences. The true teacher has a way of knowing exactly what is needed.

I discovered Ram's book, *Be Love Now*, in Village Books in Fairhaven, Washington, after facilitating a retreat at Samish Island. I stopped in to have a coffee and a look at the books, when a single book on a promotional table caught my eye. *Be Love Now* seemed to fly off the table and into my hands and heart. As I read the inside cover, I found it no coincidence that the first review was by you: "So many people are desperately searching for love, whether consciously or unconsciously. May Ram Dass's intimate and heartfelt account inspire others to find their own path of true love, compassion, and joyful service."[18] As I read this, it was as if you, my own beloved teacher, were speaking to me and encouraging me to read this book. I couldn't wait to get home and start reading!

When I finally read Ram's words, I felt a deep sense of recognition in my heart. Here was someone else who was crazy in love with his teacher, with God, and with life itself. While each guru/disciple relationship is different, so many of Ram's stories about Maharaj-ji corroborated the experience I was having with you. I was beginning to weave the precious strands of my own story into a universal love story not only for myself, but for everyone.

Maharaj-ji is known by his signature plaid blanket that is always wrapped around him. Finding this connection to Ram Dass's guru felt like the "warm blanket" feeling from my childhood when I would get down on my knees and pray. Here was the answer to some of my heartfelt prayers for understanding the nature of this vast mystical relationship of Love.

The Merging of Minds

*When I looked up into his eyes, there was only this deep
unconditional love and compassion that has remained with me
ever since...and the intimate revelation that he knew my inmost
thoughts and emotions. In truth the mind reading just softened
me up. The real thing was unconditional love.*
Ram Dass, Be Love Now

Dear Thay,

It seems that many spiritual seekers who have had an encounter with a realized spiritual master feel like their teacher can somehow read their mind. I too have had a sense that you know my thoughts. That very first time I looked into your eyes, I felt like you could see everything in me from a much larger perspective. You knew my past, my future, my thoughts, you knew me better than I knew myself, and yet it was all held in a vast field of unconditional love. You answered the question of my heart before I could even put it into words.

Last year at the retreat, there seemed to be many times you could read my mind, whether we were sitting in the forest and I asked you silently in my mind if I could take a picture, or when you looked directly at me during dharma talks as if to say "Are you getting this?" The word or phrase you were saying at the time seemed to be meant just for me, landing directly in my heart, answering a question or thought I had in my mind. This seems to be one of your many ways of transmitting the teachings and love that you embody.

God, Guru and Self Are Us

It's like having intense love for Jesus as a human being. Initially
there's dualism. Then as your love for Jesus grows, you start to
meet the Christ. Then as you love the Christ more and more, you
keep merging into that love. When you've merged fully into the
Christ, there is only One. That's the route of devotion to the guru.
You feel the presence of the inner guru and keep merging
into that presence.
Ram Dass, *Be Love Now*

Dear Thay,

One of the images that came to me as I looked into your eyes that first time, was of reaching to touch the hem of Christ's garment. Like the woman in the bible, I was changed, and transformed at deep levels in silent wordless ways. Before traveling to Plum Village, I still had what I would call a dualistic relationship with you, with Thay as my beloved teacher outside of me, and me as the student outside of Thay. Slowly, the lines are becoming more and more blurry.

One of the many gifts of a truly enlightened teacher like yourself is that there seems to be no "self" left to demand that we follow your religion or path. Truly, this experience is beyond religion. It is simply an invitation to go deeper into the great loving Mystery that holds us all. There is no sense with you that I have to become a good Buddhist in order to be your disciple. In fact, I feel like it was you, dear Thay, who pointed me back to the true living Christ within my own root tradition.

As a child I grew up with stories and teachings of Jesus, but that's all they were—stories and thoughts in my mind about a loving human being called the Son of God, who lived over two thousand years ago. In one timeless moment, you transmitted an embodied experience of the Living Buddha, Living Christ. Now, when I read the bible and other sacred scriptures, the words come alive for me. They are feelings engraved deep in my heart, my body, and my very soul, of a vast Love that cannot be put into words or confined to one religion.

Last June, not only did I feel a sense of inter-being as I watched you walk and drink your tea, I began to notice an intimate tender loving space opening in my heart center. There was a vibrant energetic aliveness that I felt, still feel, not only when I'm in your physical presence, but also when I'm at home and no longer with you and the sangha. The subtle fragrance of your love lingers in my heart, like pungent incense permeating the air.

Through my daily meditation practice and in many moments throughout the day, I have begun to consciously connect with this loving energy. Although your physical body is thousands of miles away, the outer guru and inner guru are merging in my heart. Only it isn't just you. It's the Buddha mind and the Christ consciousness merging in me. The physical form of the teacher or guru is the vessel of unconditional love that points us to that which is already within us, inseparably connected to the whole universe.

An Imaginary Friend

Now I look for his eyes everywhere...He lives as the loving, vast, all-embracing presence in which everything exists. He is the all encompassing sky that holds the earth, the stars, the clouds and the pollution. There's no place outside of Maharaj-ji for me.
Krishna Das, *Chants Of A Lifetime*

Dear Thay,

Like Ram Dass and indeed like some young children, I talk to you all the time in my mind and imagination. Perhaps this is like learning to pray unceasingly. You are my secret friend and lover. I walk for you. I invite you to feel my solid steps on the ground, to feel the warm sun on your face, the breeze in your hair (oops, monks don't have hair!) We watch together as Emma scampers ahead, sniffing away and wagging her tail in delight. I invite you to see with my eyes, listen with my ears, feel with my skin, and at the same time I pray that I might see with your eyes and listen with your ears, because we inter-are. Sometimes, I even invite you to do dishes with me, since in *Fragrant Palm Leaves* you write about how much you used to enjoy the feeling of the warm water on your hands as you did the dishes.

I must admit, sometimes I feel like I've just got an extreme case of projection. It was such a relief to read Ram Dass talk about how he uses his imagination to talk to Maharaj-ji. As Ram Dass says "our imagination is simply another level of being with the guru." Other mystics have agreed. In an online talk Ram Dass gave in 1996, he says that Maharaj-ji played with his mind, and that it was delicious to find a "playmate," because that's the gift of the guru, or a wise friend on the path. Ram says we all can have an imaginary spiritual friend, and that we can use that playmate as a vehicle to get free from our ego. You can create your own playmate by giving them the qualities that you want to cultivate, like wisdom, love, emptiness of form, a true devotional heart, etc. Is this not the practice of all the saints and mystics, as they cultivated a real and passionate love with the Christ, the Buddha, Krishna, or the Divine in their heart? Is this also not the practice of becoming filled with bodhicitta, the mind of love, and enlightenment? At its essence, it is a skillful means to embody the qualities of the great beings we love and aspire to be like, until we too can finally realize the vast mind of love.

CHAPTER 16

Happy Teachers Will Change the World

Our mission as teachers is not just to transmit knowledge, but to form human beings to construct a worthy, beautiful human race, in order to take care of our precious planet.
Thich Nhat Hanh, Happy Teachers Change the World

EDUCATORS RETREAT, AUGUST 2013, BROCK UNIVERSITY

Present Moment, Awkward Moment

August 10

Dear Thay,

I have arrived here at Brock University in St. Catharines, a vibrant city between Toronto and Niagara Falls, for the Educators Retreat. As a volunteer, I have the luxury of arriving one day early. Doug will arrive tomorrow, after dropping our son Andrew off to catch a bus to a youth camp sponsored by our church. I am excited to be sharing this retreat with my husband, but I'm also happy for this first day on my own to settle in.

Later that evening, there is a special dinner for all the volunteers, and we are given a coveted orange T-shirt with your calligraphy "Happy Teachers Will Change the World." Yes, that says it all! We must begin to teach these mindfulness practices to the next generation. Teaching children is a sacred trust. It begins with teachers who have learned to slow down and take care of themselves, so they can create moments of mindfulness in their classrooms. Kids and teachers are so over-stimulated and stressed out these days: they need mindfulness practices to help them feel and release difficult emotions. What a beautiful vision you have for the energy of mindfulness to permeate the entire world. It truly takes a village, and teachers are such a key part of our global village.

On Sunday the campus is transformed into a busy beehive of activity as over thirteen hundred educators, pre-school teachers to university professors from all over North America and the world, begin to arrive. I am assigned to a group with Sister True Dedication to help give directions and show people to their dorm room. She reminds us to be mindful ourselves as we welcome people, inviting them into a slower rhythm of living and being. Every so often the bell sounds, and we all stop and breathe, creating a small oasis of calm in the midst of busy arrivals. As I take slow measured steps, showing people to their rooms, I can sense the busy impatient energy that most people bring to a retreat like this. Slowing down is not easy. I remember how restless I felt during the first few days of the 2011 retreat in Vancouver. Now, I'm so grateful for these five-day retreats as an opportunity to slow down and create a new habit of living life fully and consciously, instead of the busy distracted lives most of us live.

It's an exhausting endless day, filled with myriad details that need to be attended to in getting thirteen hundred people settled in. When I finally get back to our room, Doug has arrived, and I fall into his arms with a big sigh. It's so good to have him here and to be able to share this retreat with him. I can't wait for him to meet you.

Having stayed to the very end to assist people, we ended up being late for supper, then almost late for your orientation dharma talk. By the time we arrive, the cavernous room is completely full. We spot a few spaces to sit about halfway up, so make our way there, but are told we have to keep the aisle free. As we try to get up, the bell sounds. Of course at Plum Village retreats, when the bell sounds, you stop right where we are. So here we are in the very centre of the room holding an awkward position, not quite sitting and not quite standing. I turn my head and look at you sideways. You have the most amused look on your face, with that twinkle of laughter in your eyes. "Hello, my dear teacher. I'm almost here!"

With standing room only, we finally find a place to stand at the back of the room. All we can see are the backs of other bodies on tippy toes, and people craning their necks to see, just like us. I close my eyes and come back to my breath. I can't see you, but I can hear your gentle voice inviting us to come home to ourselves, to hold our suffering like a mother holds her baby. So I hold my tiredness and frustration of not being able to see, and somehow I listen at a deeper level. As the frustration dissolves, a feeling of gratitude enfolds me. I'm truly here, along with my beloved husband. He's so kind and patient, not upset by the crowd around us. I can feel the connection between his heart and mine. I feel the connection with your great loving heart, dear Thay. Somehow we are all contained in this vast loving heart.

Your Wondrous Soft Eyes

You are a shy divine deer that I cannot cease tracking. Though only once of late did I get so close to see my own face and heart reflected in your wondrous soft eyes.
Hafiz

August 12
Dear Thay,
This morning I got up very early to take a slow leisurely walk by myself. I dressed quietly so as not to wake Doug, and followed the long maze of hallways until I was outside the dormitory. Even here atop the Niagara Escarpment, the sun isn't quite up yet, although I can see the first few rays of light beginning to peak above the horizon. I take a deep breath, savouring the quietness of these pre-dawn moments, before the rest of the world awakens. My thoughts turn to you. I wonder where you are staying. Do you sleep well at these retreats, especially after traveling so far? Are you already up at this early hour, sitting deep in meditation? Secretly, I fantasize about somehow encountering you on one of the many paths that encircle this campus. What would I do or say?

I'm not familiar with the campus, but I finally find a small path that seems to lead into a wooded area, where I fall into the familiar rhythm of my own breath in touch with each step. The path winds deeper into the forest. I have no idea where I am headed. All of a sudden a beautiful deer appears out of nowhere, standing right in front of me. I have no idea where it came from, or why it didn't run away. Perhaps it felt my peaceful steps. We both stand very still looking into each other's eyes. It is another sacred moment. Time stands still, as we stand still, lost in each other's gaze. Finally, with one last look, the deer bounds away.

Later, I read in one of your books that the Buddha was said to appear sometimes as a deer. It seems like magical thinking. Yet, perhaps I have seen the Buddha. Perhaps I have seen you. Perhaps I have seen myself.

My Two Beloveds

After our experience of being late for your dharma talk last night, Doug and I arrive extra early this morning so we can find a place close to the front, where we can see you. With the doors not yet open, we find ourselves waiting in a large crowd of people, all with the same thought and intention. Finally, the door opens and a swell of people swarms into the room. I try to be mindful, but my steps are much faster than usual. I so want to be close to you Thay, and I so want Doug to be close to you too. I hope he will have the same chance to look into your eyes of love, like I did in Vancouver.

As the bell sounds, you invite us to listen with every cell of our body. You remind us that our mother and father and ancestors are present in every cell of our body, so they are listening with us. It's a powerful feeling, as over thirteen hundred people, most of them teachers and educators, breathe and listen and settle in together. I think of our two sons, Andrew and Brendan, and am filled with hope that the world we have inherited from our parents and grandparents can be healed and transformed by this powerful energy of mindfulness.

Doug and I sit together for your first dharma talk. I sit still, breathing and calling to you silently in my mind as I did at Plum Village. At one point, you look over and we make eye contact. Here I sit with my beloved husband beside me, and my beloved teacher standing in front of me. I silently ask you to bless Doug, to bless our marriage. Your answering smile is the blessing. My two lovers have met. I sit here between them, embraced by both. My heart feels like it will burst.

Growing Into My True Self

There are things that the Buddha or Jesus said thousands of years
ago; they may begin only now to have an effect.
Thich Nhat Hanh, *The Raft Is Not the Shore*

August 13
Dear Thay,
Today you started your dharma talk with the children by sharing a dream you had over twenty years ago. I always find it so touching that a respected Zen master like yourself is so willing to share more personal aspects of your life. Perhaps that's what speaks most deeply to my heart, and why your personal stories seem to contain the deepest teaching.

The children gather around you near the front, occasionally giggling as you sprinkle the re-telling with your unique and well-timed humour. You dreamed that you had been accepted into a prestigious class at college with a very distinguished professor. As you entered the classroom, you noticed a younger version of yourself that looked exactly like you, also entering the class. It was confusing. Was that you or not you? The lady in the office told you "You have definitely been accepted, but not him." The subject of the class was music, which seemed a bit strange as you did not have much musical experience. When you got to the classroom, you were surprised to find thousands of people there. What an honour it was to be in that class. You were told that you would be the first to give a presentation, and you wondered what you could share. Nervously, as you felt in your pocket, you found a bell (surprise!) and thought "I can do that!" Then just as they were announcing the professor's arrival, you woke up!

Dreams often contain messages from our deep unconscious, or perhaps from universal consciousness. Dreams often bring something to the surface, to be seen and expressed and learned from. Your own interpretation of this dream was that perhaps the young man was an earlier version of you, still caught in certain kinds of views and not yet free enough to be accepted into a master class. Your older self had attained some insight that allowed you to free yourself from attachment.

As I look back on my own life, I can see many places where I have been stuck in my point of view. Raised in a Christian community in the sixties, at that time we were taught not only that Christianity was the only path, but that we were the "one true church." And of course, only men could be ordained to the priesthood because Jesus only had men as his twelve disciples! As a rebellious teenager I began to question those beliefs, especially as I started to interact with friends from other faiths and traditions. It no longer made sense to me that God would limit Herself to just one faith (or one gender!) Thankfully, my Christian community has also evolved beyond the notion of being the only path, and now welcomes and honours believers from many different traditions. It seems that religions can also move beyond their younger self of outdated structures and rigid beliefs, to a more mature and wise self. Still, structural and systemic change is much slower, and often painful for all involved. Many people are confined to rigid belief patterns often imposed by outer authority figures.

Over time, and with the practice of yoga and meditation, my heart has expanded beyond the words and scriptures and beliefs that define any one religion, to the unity that lies beneath the surface, especially in the mystical streams of most religions. So I find myself now sitting in a retreat organized by my Buddhist community with my husband by my side, and my Buddhist teacher smiling in front.

We have a dear friend at this retreat, also ordained as a minister in our church, so it seems my two communities are coming together. I look around this gathering and imagine there are many people with Christian roots and connections, some still involved, others looking for something they haven't found in the religion of their birth.

In your first dharma talk you said "A flower is made of non-flower elements...the sun, the soil, the rain, the gardener. You cannot take the sun out of the flower. They inter-are! Buddhism too is made of non-Buddhist elements." I can see the Buddha and his roots in the Hindu religion, and the many monks and nuns and practitioners through two thousand years, each bringing their own insight and flavour. Buddhism has also changed and adapted as it has taken root in different countries. Even yourself, dear Thay, coming from a long lineage of Buddhist teachers, has been deeply touched by your encounters with respected Christian teachers in the western world, like Martin Luther King, Thomas Merton, and Daniel Berrigan.

I feel this merging deep in my soul, as I feel the many streams of my life coming together in this moment. I feel the Living Buddha and Living Christ coming together in me. I can still feel the young idealistic Christian girl that I was growing up, with the seed of faith planted in her heart, thanks to the generations before her. I can also feel the woman I have become now, with a deep longing in my heart to create bridges of understanding and spiritual practice between different religions.

When I received the Five Mindfulness Trainings in a formal ceremony in Vancouver just two years ago, I was given the dharma name "Divine Oneness of the Heart." How did you know this was the deepest desire and volition of my life, when I didn't even know it fully myself? It is a mystery, along with all the other questions have about this spiritual relationship with you that defies conventions and easy answers. I am learning to trust in the not knowing and slowly growing into the possibilities of that name. I am different from the girl I was, growing up. I am different from the grieving woman who looked into your eyes in

Vancouver. I have been accepted into the great universal classroom of Life, with a wise teacher who cannot be defined by any one form or religion. I have nothing to offer, no bell in my pocket, just a heart that is longing for a Love beyond form.

We Draw the Circle Together

Drink your tea slowly and reverently, as if it is the axis on which the whole earth revolves – slowly, evenly, without rushing toward the future.
Thich Nhat Hanh, *The Miracle of Mindfulness*

August 14
Dear Thay,
Once again your dharma talk begins this morning by speaking directly to the children gathered around you. It is such a precious time. I often get more out of the dharma talks to the children than from the adult version of your talk. Perhaps I'm still a child myself on this spiritual journey. Your use of stories and symbols speaks deeply to the child in me.

You begin by holding up your cup of tea and with that mischievous smile on your face, ask the children "Can you see the cloud in this tea?" Can we see how the tea contains water that had fallen as rain from a cloud way up in the sky? All things, including people are in constant transformation, even as we try to hold on to our bodies, our thoughts, our beliefs, our loved ones, our own life. If we are in constant transformation, there really can be no birth, no death, only change and continuation in another form.

Next you hold up a piece of parchment paper that contains just an empty zen circle with no words. Again with that same mischievous smile you say "There is a cloud in this circle too!...I'm going to let you in on one of my secrets." We all lean in a bit closer to hear your quiet voice tell us your secret. "Thay always drinks tea while he is doing his calligraphy, and he always mixes some of his tea with the Chinese ink I use. So the cloud is there."

"Here is another secret. When Thay draws, he is always in touch with his breath." You place your finger at the bottom of the circle like an imaginary brush. "Thay always breathes in as he traces a circle from the bottom to the top, then he breathes out as he completes the circle moving downwards on the other side." I naturally match my breath to your words and movements. Somehow it connects me in a deep visceral way to this teaching. I can almost feel the paintbrush in my own hand as I breathe in and out.

When Thay breathes in and out, he smiles to relax, and calligraphy becomes a meditation of peace, joy, and communion with the whole Cosmos. I invite the whole sangha, the monks and nuns and laypersons to breathe and draw with me. So now you can see the sangha in this circle. Thay invites his teacher and all his ancestors to breathe and draw the circle with him. So Thay is in touch with his ancestors, his friends and disciples, the ink, the tea, the cloud... It is a deep form of meditation.
Thich Nhat Hanh, Dharma Talk[19]

As I sit and breathe, I can feel the reality of this simple yet intricate teaching in the depths of my being. You are transmitting something so much more than just the spoken word. I can feel the whole sangha, all of us breathing and sitting together here. I can feel you, dear Thay, and the long lineage of teachers who have lovingly preserved and expanded these teachings. I can feel Doug sitting beside me, our parents, our grandparents, our ancestors, our children, and grandchildren yet to be. They are all here. The ink, the tea, the cloud...both the emptiness and fullness of the circle you are holding up are all drawing us together in this moment. Once more, we have had a small taste of the inter-being you embody.

The Unwritten Curriculum

The unwritten curriculum in the classroom is the teacher's
presence, dissolving the boundaries of teacher and student.
Meena Srinivasan

Dear Thay,
The theme of this retreat is based on one of your calligraphies, "Happy Teachers Will Change the World." Your deepest insights seem to make themselves known first through your paintbrush. You are well aware that many teachers and educators are so overworked and stressed out, they have nothing left to give back to their students. We all need these practices of sitting and breathing and walking and deep relaxation to release the tension from our bodies, to calm our minds, and to simply take time to be with the many feelings we're usually too busy to attend to.

I'm beginning to sense a small part of the huge vision you have for re-imagining and creating a more peaceful world. A dharma friend of mine says you have a two-thousand-year vision and beyond! That vision begins with our children and grandchildren, who will continue us into the future. That vision starts in the classroom, by addressing the needs of the whole child.

Children are so welcome at your retreats, and your monks and nuns provide such loving attention, teaching the practices of mindfulness in age-appropriate ways. I love to watch you interacting with the children. It's almost like you become a child yourself and know exactly how to keep their attention, whether telling a story about a dream, or showing how to invite the bell, or how you paint your calligraphies. The love you have for children is so evident in every single word and gesture, and the childlike wonder reflected in your eyes.

At this Retreat for Mindfulness in Education, in addition to your own dharma talks, we have had short talks by many esteemed teachers and educators sharing new and innovative ways of bringing mindfulness and healing into our schools and universities at every level. We have learned how to educate for the whole person by integrating social and emotional intelligence into the classroom. We have learned how mindfulness practices can enhance the presence of the teacher, dissolving the usual boundaries between teacher and student for better communication. We have learned how the simple practices of inviting the bell or deep relaxation in the classroom can help integrate a student's body, mind, heart and brain, and to cultivate the capacity for deeper attention. Some speakers spoke of how bringing mindfulness into the classroom can help students deal with their feelings, and perhaps past traumas. Even making simple changes in the way classrooms are set up, like putting desks in circles instead of rows, can create an atmosphere that fosters connection instead of separation. There are so many possibilities. I'm starting to get a sneak peek at the kind of vision you have to bring more happiness, well-being and peace not only to teachers and students but to all levels of society, for generations to come.

Your Vulnerable Heart

When a sage is there and you sit near him, you feel light,
you feel peace.
Thich Nhat Hanh, *The Raft Is Not the Shore*

August 15

Dear Thay,

Today before your dharma talk, Brother Nhuyen is playing his guitar and leading us in the Breathing Song. "In, out, deep, slow, calm, ease, smile, release. Present moment, Wonderful Moment." The children are gathered around him, up on the stage singing earnestly with exuberant energy. Each child is seen and valued as an important part of this community. I'm sure each child senses this open and welcoming way of being. Brother Nhuyen has such a beautiful smile. He exudes the same inner joy and peace that you do. At times during this retreat, I've seen him acting as your personal attendant, carrying the bag that contains your books, or making sure your tea is ready. Each simple action seems to be an act of service and love for his teacher. I see his love for you in his eyes. I wonder what it would be like to spend so much time close to you, attending to your daily needs, but at the same time just quietly absorbing the peaceful energy that seems to permeate the very air you breathe. I can sense your presence in this gentle and kind monk.

Just as he's about to start guiding us in meditation, he looks over to the side of the stage and says with such joy in his voice "Our teacher has arrived." And indeed you have. The small bell rings, and we all stand up to greet you, our beloved teacher.

Today's dharma talk of Questions and Answers reminds me of the timeless moment in Vancouver, receiving your gaze and transmission of love. Today, I am content to sit here with Doug by my side. I have no burning questions.

As usual, you invite the children up on stage to ask their questions first. A little boy in a blue T-Shirt and shorts nimbly climbs onto the adult-sized chair and asks a short question in French. Though you speak fluent French, Sister Pine translates so we can all understand. "Will you sing us a song?" The hall erupts in joyful laughter. There is a long silent pause as you sit quietly, then a well-timed clearing of your throat. You tell a short story of a song from your own childhood, then in a soft shy voice, begin to sing in French. It is a touching moment with a revered and wise Zen Master willing to show a more vulnerable side of himself. In an instant, you are transformed from an eighty-seven-year-old monk to a young Vietnamese boy singing a song from his childhood. I feel the innocence in this young boy's heart. I feel the innocence in my teacher's heart, still as open as a lotus blossom, even after a lifetime lived in the war-torn country of his youth, the constant rebuilding of bombed-out villages, and finally the exile from his beloved homeland.

We Breathe As One

August 16

Dear Thay,

Today you began your dharma talk with this beautiful meditation on inter-being:

> *Breathing in, I invite my father to breathe with me.*
> *Breathing out, father and daughter are one...*
> *Breathing in, I feel free.*
> *Breathing out, I feel light.*
> *Father do you feel free and light?*

I think of my father, who died almost ten years ago. Gerald was a gentle man who was often content to simply sit and enjoy the sun, or quietly read the paper. Originally trained as a pharmacist, he soon came out from behind the counter to travel for large pharmaceutical companies. His territory often included small towns, where he would patiently wait for the pharmacist behind the counter to finally look up and give him his attention. Although they spoke about current drugs and therapies, the conversation would often turn to other things, like family, or events happening in the community. My dad was always a good listener, and never in a hurry. He loved to hear other people's stories. This morning I can feel my father in me. He's not really gone. He's here breathing in me. I too have the capacity to just sit and enjoy the warmth of the sun on my face. I too love to listen to other people's stories. I too have a story to tell. Father and daughter are one.

Breathing in, I invite my mother to breathe with me.
Breathing out, mother and daughter enjoy breathing together.
This body is mine, but it is also yours, mother.
Let us breathe peacefully.
Breathing in, I feel so light. Breathing out, I feel so free.
Mother do you feel free and light?

Now, my thoughts turn to my mother. It's been two years, but my heart still feels a bit fragile when I think of her. I can still see her bustling about her kitchen. Like many women of her generation, being a homemaker was an important part of her personality. She loved to bake and make people feel welcome. She had a deep faith that sustained her even in her darkest moments. She planted that seed of faith in all three of her children, and each of us have found ways of nurturing it in our own way.

It is because of the seed of my mother's faith planted in me that I now find myself at a Buddhist retreat. Yet my mother's faith was limited to one God, one religion, one way of believing. So as I sit and breathe with my mother here, I feel her presence and her DNA in my body. I breathe with her. I breathe for her, as her continuation from a faith limited in one time and place to a faith not limited to one religion or set of beliefs. I feel light. I feel free.

Breathing in, I invite Jesus to breathe with me.
Breathing out, I invite Buddha to breathe with me.
Jesus and me, Buddha and me.

Not only my biological ancestors are breathing in me, but my spiritual ancestors are breathing in me. I can feel the Christ breathing in me, beyond the confines of the Christian religion founded in his name. I can feel the Christ who wants to break down the boundaries that divide people and cultures and religions. I can feel the Buddha breathing in me, and all the way down the long lineage of teachers to you, dear Thay, breathing in me. Living Buddha, living Christ, two streams coming together in me. I reach out and touch Doug's hand and our eyes meet in the recognition of this moment. I can feel the streams of his ancestors coming together in our lives, woven together through the many moments of love intertwined and pouring out into the vessel of this sacred moment. I smile at this thought, and watch as a smile blooms and radiates from your face, dear Thay.

CHAPTER 17

Healing Inter-Generational Suffering

"FINDING OUR TRUE HOME" RETREAT.
OCTOBER 11 – 16, 2013. DEER PARK MONASTERY,

Peace Begins With Your Lovely Smile

October 10
Dear Thay,

It's fall, and a few red leaves are hanging precariously on the lonely oak trees standing against the Chapparal Mountains of southern California. Yet with the heat waves sweltering off the ground here at Deer Park Monastery, it doesn't feel like fall, and I know the clothes I packed will be much too warm. Perspiration trickles down my brow, as I meet a nun in her heavy brown robes climbing the long set of stairs from the dining area. She too is perspiring, but her peaceful smile reminds me to come back to the beauty all around me.

I gaze out at the panoramic view and notice a long building with a curved roof beneath the dining area. Deer Park Monastery seems to be built into the side of a steep hill, making the sparse living quarters, office area, dining area, and the meditation hall all on different levels. One has to be in good shape to live here and do several sets of stairs many times a day. I picture you even at eighty-seven, steadily climbing these stairs, just like you climbed the steep hill at New Hamlet.

I descend another steep set of stairs to the Ocean of Peace meditation hall. Off to the side stands a gazebo housing the large bell that announces the beginning and close of each day. I take off my shoes, then step into the coolness of the large cathedral-like space. The retreat has not started yet, and I am met by rows of brown mats and meditation cushions inviting me to a deeper journey into myself. At the very front, behind the altar, is one of your many calligraphies "This Is It." I take a deep breath and feel the meaning of these words penetrate my body. This is it. This moment is it. This breath is it. Another calligraphy off to the side says "Peace begins with your lovely smile." A smile brushes my own lips, as I think about your lovely smile. Perhaps our smiles reflec each other. It feels like you've left secret messages all around, not just for me, but for all of us to remember. I can't wait to see your lovely smile again.

Flow Like a River

One drop of water will not arrive at the ocean. One drop of water will evaporate along the way. But if the drop of water joins the river, then the whole river will go to the ocean.
Thich Nhat Hanh, *Awakening of the Heart*

October 11
Happy Birthday Dear Thay,
Or perhaps I should say "Happy Continuation Day," as you say in the Plum Village tradition. You teach "there is no birth, there is no death," that we simply slip in and out of different forms. What a joy it is to be with you again in your now eighty-seven year old form. How fortunate I am to be able to spend time with you at two retreats this year, first the Educators Retreat in Canada, and now this. I feel like a Thay groupie, following you from retreat to retreat like a teen-ager following a rock star, concert to concert! I smile at this thought, since this is definitely not a wild rock concert, but rather a journey into the wildness of my own heart. And I am not a young teen, but a mature woman, filled with a passionate love she cannot explain for her teacher, for the Buddha, for the Christ, for God, for life. Although my body has aged, my heart can still do somersaults.

For this first orientation session, I've found a cushion close to the front, close to you. As I sit quietly watching my breath, the meditation hall seems unusually noisy. Many people here at Deer Park seem to know each other, greeting and embracing each other as if they haven't seen each other in a very long time. Even though we are supposed to be quiet, they talk animatedly, eager to catch up. I am reminded of retreats and camps in my own church community and the sense of connectedness. I feel a deep sense of gratitude to be part of both these sanghas. I feel at home in both.

Finally, the room begins to hush as you slowly glide in, and we all stand with reverence for our beloved teacher. A bell sounds and we bring our hands together and bow. Softly in my own heart, I whisper "Happy Continuation Day, Thay. I offer you my utmost love and devotion. May your love continue in me." As we settle back onto our cushions, you invite us to relax and enjoy our breathing and togetherness as a sangha. "Breathing in, I am alive. Breathing out I smile to life both inside and out." Today we celebrate you and your life, dear teacher. We cherish these simple practices that are slowly deepening in all of us. They are such a precious gift, to ourselves and to each other. Breathing together like this creates a powerful collective energy that nourishes each one of us, and ultimately the world.

As usual at the beginning of a retreat, you invite all the monks and nuns of Plum Village to come forward and chant to Avalokiteshvara, the bodhisattva of deep listening and compassion. As we are held and bathed in this collective energy of compassion, we also send compassion out to friends and loved ones who are suffering at this time, and ultimately out to the whole world. You say it's not exactly like praying to a divine power, but rather generating the energy of compassion to nourish and heal the world. Perhaps that is the difference between Christian prayer and Buddhist meditation. Maybe it's just the words we use, and the intention behind the words. The energy and source are the same.

A young monk strums the guitar, and it feels like each sound is gently plucking at my heartstrings. I feel a tender resonance in my heart centre, as a nun adds to the mournful melody on the violin. The voices of all the monks and nuns now blend together in this universal chant to

Avalokiteshvara, inviting each of us to touch our own suffering, and to be embraced by the energy of the sangha. The chant is punctuated by a drum and occasional bells, while your graceful hand mudras seem to focus and send the energy directly from your heart to ours. My heart feels so open and tender. I remember that the solitary tear I felt at the end of the 21-Day Retreat seemed to contain the energy of a shared suffering transformed into caring and compassion for all. Both suffering and compassion seem to flow together.

How Do I Listen?

October 12

Dear Thay,

This morning during meditation I am sitting in the very front row, directly in front of you. I am a bit nervous at first, remembering moments when you seem to be able to read my mind, but I soon settle into the rhythm of my own breath. I can feel the solid focused energy that exudes from your peaceful presence. You seem to be holding the whole sangha in this silent stream.

> *Breathing in I know I am breathing in,*
> *Breathing out I know I am breathing out.*
> *Breathing in, I follow my breath all the way in,*
> *Breathing out, I follow my breath all the way out.*
> *Breathing in, I am aware of my whole body,*
> *Breathing out, I relax my whole body.*
> *Present moment, Wonderful moment.*
> **Thich Nhat Hanh,** *Breathing Gatha*

Every so often the bell sounds, as if to invite us deeper into this silent space with you. It feels like my whole body is alive and shimmering with the vibration of the bell. My mind is peaceful. My heart is soft. My heart is awake to yours.

My heart is still awake to yours when I return for your dharma talk. Once more, I find a cushion close to where you sit on your cushion on a raised podium that is framed by an elegant spray of pink and white orchids. Before you begin your dharma talk, you sit very still, slowly turning your head from side to side, your eyes taking in the vast sea of people gathered here from all over North America and the world. Your eyes flicker, as if an outward manifestation of an inner process of listening and tuning into the energy of the room. It's as if you are sifting through layer after layer of thoughts and feelings to see our suffering, to see our joy, to see our past, to see our future. Perhaps that's why your dharma talks seem to speak directly to each of us in our own way, while also speaking to the collective suffering and joy we all carry.

Finally, as your face lights up with your signature smile and your eyes refocus and soften, you begin. "Good morning, dear sangha, today is Saturday, October 12 in the year 2013. We are in the second day of our retreat with the theme of Finding Our True Home at Deer Park Monastery. I can't seem to help myself, but to stare deep into your eyes as you speak. I want to listen with more than just my ears. Somehow my eyes have become part of my listening. It feels as if every cell of my body is awake, awaiting the vibration of your voice. I remember the first time I looked into your eyes, in Vancouver. There's a similar quality of attention, of listening beyond the outer meaning of the words. The soothing timbre of your voice encourages me to lean in with my body, to listen to your voice the same way I listen to the bell.

The Better Way to Live Alone

Your dharma talk was on the Sutra on the Better Way of Living Alone, and how the Buddha taught the practice of solitude, but not so as to abandon society. You told the story of a monk that misunderstood and did everything alone. Avoiding others, he grew proud of his practice.

This is not what the Buddha had in mind. The Buddha spoke of another way of living alone, not actually isolating oneself but knowing how to come home to one's breath, one's body, one's true home.

Since meeting you, I intentionally seek more silence and solitude in my life, away from the usual social conventions. I am an introvert. It's one of the reasons I've come to this retreat. Yet, this retreat is not exactly silent. There seems to be more talking than at other retreats I've attended. Not everyone is observing the Noble Silence listed on the schedule. I try to be patient, but I become irritated. Like the monk in your story, I become judgmental, yet I feel compassion for him, as if he too was just yearning for some time to be quiet and alone with himself, away from the challenges of community. He had a deep volition to practice, and there doesn't seem to be anything wrong with that. While I understand the need for a loving community, I also feel there are times when we have to draw away, to be by ourselves.

I have learned much in solitude. I have learned much from loneliness. Christian writer Henri Nouwen says "Solitude is the ground from which community grows."[20] It is only when we know how to be comfortable by ourselves in solitude that we can truly be there for each other in community. Indeed, spending quiet time away from others, especially in nature, opens me to a different way of relating to the world. Sitting alone in the middle of a forest or by a river, a tender intimacy with life opens me to greater intimacy with myself, and ultimately with others. I come back refreshed, ready to interact and listen to others in a more loving way.

Always needing to talk can be exhausting. Spending time in silence in community allows us to rest and be there for each other, and leads to an intimacy that is deeper than words. Silence does not depend on words or actions or gestures to communicate. A wordless transmission takes place in a community that knows how to be silent together. It is the same silent transmission I feel, just being in your presence.

I am learning so much beyond words. Yet words are important. Every word you say conveys a message that can be understood both individually and collectively. Interpreting the story about the monk, you said "to live alone means not to have a second person living inside us. Most of us live with two people, the one we are, and the one we think we should be." Wow. It seems you've looked inside my skin and seen both people living in me. You know human nature so well.

Who do I think I should be? What am I striving for? Ever since that timeless moment of looking into your eyes, I am filled with desire and craving for another once-in-a-lifetime moment, a moment that has left me wanting more. It's like an addiction. I never seem to be satisfied. I follow you from one retreat to another, sitting in the front row, hoping for a look here, a word there, a smile, an acknowledgement, maybe even enlightenment. I want to follow your finger straight to the moon.

Then, sometimes with just one breath, that striving person dissolves, and there is just the gentle breeze brushing my skin, the eagle soaring in the vast blue sky above. Time flows effortlessly, without my trying to control it. I can be myself. I can allow others to be themselves. I can let go of trying to attain something in the future. I can let go of the planning. I can let go of all the preconceived notions I have about my spiritual path or enlightenment. I can look into my teacher's eyes and see myself perfectly reflected there. I already know the better way to live alone. I just need to keep remembering, and loving the part of me that forgets.

Later in your talk, you talked about volition. As our eyes met, you smiled and said "Volition is your deepest desire and aspiration. It gives you a lot of energy." That energy has lit a holy passion in my heart, a spark that keeps growing brighter as it joins with other sparks. It feels as if you know that the deepest desire of my heart is to dissolve into the oneness with God and creation that all saints and mystics speak of. You know my deep desire to be a bridge of understanding between different religions and spiritual traditions. Through this mystical relationship, you seem to be teaching me the true nature of inter-being.

The Tears You Cried Yesterday Have Become Rain

There are those of us who need a certain dose of suffering in order to be able to recognize happiness. But there are those of us who don't need to suffer, and yet still have the capacity to know that "not suffering" is happiness. With mindfulness we become aware of the suffering that's going on around us.
Thich Nhat Hanh, *Buddha Mind, Buddha Body*

October 13

Dear Thay,

I never did get to ask you the "question of my heart" when I was on stage with you in Vancouver, in 2011. All my questions seemed to dissolve into the depth of your gaze. My question had something to do with suffering, but was difficult to put into words. In that quiet, vulnerable state, my heart felt tender, raw, and yet, despite my mother's recent death, there was no overwhelming sense of grief, no torrent of tears that most people feel with the loss of a loved one, especially one's mother.

Sometimes I wonder if I have small tear ducts? My eyes get moist, and sometimes a few stray tears leak out, but I have never experienced the kind of inconsolable grief that consumes body and mind. I have had no dark night of the soul. Do we need a dark night of the soul to become enlightened? Must we be completely overwhelmed by the dark in order to see the light?

Do you cry, dear Thay? Even as people tell you their deepest pain and trauma, I've never seen tears in your eyes, only compassion. You always seem so calm and serene, yet you have lived through the ravages of war in Vietnam, and exile from your homeland and the loss of your mother, and the violent death of your own beloved monks and nuns. Yesterday, towards the end of your dharma talk, you reminded us that the Buddha suffered even after he became enlightened. Teachers, you said, suffer for their disciples. That seems to be a lot of suffering to hold, even in your great heart.

I've had no major tragedies or trauma, yet my life is not untouched by sickness and death. I've felt my brother's grief as he and his wife mourned the death of their three-year-old daughter, Emma Sue, from spinal meningitis. I've felt the anguish and worry for our own two-year-old, Andrew, after a blood vessel bursting in his brain caused clusters of unexplained seizures. I've felt my mother's pain, as the ovarian cancer slowly extinguished the spark from her once-vibrant eyes. No, I am no stranger to suffering. Yet I have not been overwhelmed or debilitated by it. No torrent of gut-wrenching tears, just the slow trickle of a stream meandering through the forest of my life.

One of your famous calligraphies says "No Mud, No Lotus," and in your dharma talks you often say "You can't grow a lotus without the mud." Sometimes I wonder if I have enough mud to grow a beautiful lotus. It sounds like a silly question when there is so much suffering in our world. I don't need to create more suffering. Yet still I wonder, what mud still lurks beneath the surface of my seemingly peaceful mind? What murky water still flows through my veins from previous generations and their suffering? How do I dig into it? Is it something I can release with practice, or is it simply trusting and being with whatever arises in its own time?

Suffering is a major theme at most of your retreats. In the safe and caring container of our smaller dharma-sharing groups, people feel free to share their stories of deep suffering and trauma caused by alcoholism, abuse, mental illness, broken relationships, inconsolable grief, and all the day-to-day suffering that is part of being human. I listen deeply and feel a tender flower of compassion growing in my heart. Still, sometimes I wonder whether I have truly dealt with my own suffering.

Morning Meditation

Breathing in, I see myself as a five-year-old girl,
Breathing out, I smile to my five-year-old self.

Breathing in, I see the five-year-old girl hurt and vulnerable,
Breathing out, I embrace my five-year-old self.

Breathing in, I see my mother as a five-year-old girl,
Breathing out, I smile to my mother as a young girl.
Breathing in, I see my mother hurt and vulnerable,
Breathing out, I embrace my five-year-old mother.

Dear Thay,

This morning in our meditation practice, we were guided to see ourselves as a five-year-old child, then imagine our mother and father at the same innocent age. I can see my mother out on the old farm in the dust bowl of the Alberta prairies after the 1930's stock market crash. Her father had died of leukemia when she was just two, leaving my grandmother to raise seven girls all by herself, working her fingers to the bone to try and keep the family farm.

As the youngest of seven, my mother, Patricia, was the one who had to sleep with her mother, in the same bed where her father and mother used to sleep. After the death of her father, my mother would lie absolutely still in the darkness, listening to the sounds of my grandmother crying and sobbing. It was all too much for a young girl at such a tender age, so my mother would turn her back and hug her tiny limbs to block out the sound. There they lay, two grieving souls, lying back-to-back without touching. This was a very strong memory for my mother, who always regretted not turning towards her mother and hugging her with her tiny arms.

As my mother lay dying, she shared this painful story with me. I received it back into my heart. I wondered if my mother's pain could still be present in me? Do I have the tendency to hold back the tears, or turn away from pain instead of facing it? Or have these practices of breathing and sensing and feeling slowly been transforming this ancestral pain into understanding and compassion for my own generational pain, while the healing flows forwards to future generations? The tears my mother cried yesterday have become rain.

We Hold Our Issues in Our Tissues

Dear Thay,

I find myself saying "we hold our issues in our tissues" when teaching yoga. It seems like a trite and over-simplified phrase, but it carries a lot of truth. Similarly, you often say that our mother and father are present in every cell of our body. I think most people understand this at some level. Just like "we are what we eat," we are also what we think or have experienced. You've been talking about the Four Nutrients: edible food, sense impressions, volition, and consciousness. We are always consuming through our mouth, our eyes, our nose, our body, our mind. We have to be careful what we are consuming so we are feeding and nourishing our love, instead of suffering. All of our memories, all our feelings, are stored in our body. As a yoga teacher I know this deep in my bones, but I also know that we are complicated beings with lifetimes of feelings to be felt and healed and expressed.

I still sense there's more under the surface for me, and I want to go deeper to understand. I want to release any feelings that might be blocked. I know that the unconscious part of me wants to stay in the dark, making this a deep and difficult practice.

When you talk about consciousness in your dharma talks, you divide consciousness into "mind" and "store." You compare mind consciousness to the living room, where we entertain guests, and store consciousness to the basement, where we hide everything we don't want visitors to see. Mind consciousness is our everyday conscious mind, and store consciousness is our unconscious mind. There are many seeds that lie in our unconscious basement, both wholesome and unwholesome.

Sometimes, feelings of sadness or anger can arise in me out of the blue. I know these feelings arise from my own past experiences, but they can also arise from the experiences of past generations stored in my cellular memory. You teach that if the seed of sadness or grief has arisen from the basement of our store consciousness into our mind consciousness, our practice is to gently embrace it with our seed of mindfulness and compassion, and help it return to the basement. Each time we do this it becomes weaker and will no longer have control over us, whereas if we continue to feed these negative thoughts and feelings, they will continue to appear in our living room and act out in uncontrollable ways. Perhaps my slowly seeping tears are my gentle way of moving through different layers of grief over many years.

I know I need to hold these practices lightly. Sometimes I get so attached or caught up in how to do a practice right, or in comparing my practice to others that I forget to follow my own intuition. Too often, I allow other people's thoughts and opinions to overshadow my own knowing. True discernment and practice allow me to tune into my own inner knowing.

When We Know How to Suffer, We Suffer Much Less

Dear Thay,

Since starting yoga over twenty years ago, this ancient spiritual practice has been slowly weaving itself into the fabric of my life. Like many, I originally thought yoga was a set of postures and exercises to stay healthy and flexible. Over the years, I have learned it is so much more. It's a practice that has completely transformed my life. Perhaps that's why I so resonate with you and these practices. Breathing. Walking. Listening. Deep relaxation. It is the Plum Village yoga practice of embodied movement, breath and inter-being.

Through yoga I have fallen in love with the intimacy of my own breath, and with the mystery that same breath points to. Through yoga I have connected to my body in a loving way, learning to pay attention to subtle sensations I would not have been aware of in the past. Through yoga I have learned to recognize and be with tension and discomfort in my physical body. Through yoga I have learned how to breathe into and be with feelings of anger or frustration or sadness. Instead of a practice, yoga has become a way of inhabiting my body and my life.

It's simply a way of being, and this way of being led me to you.

One of the practices that has brought much healing to my own life, and that of my students, is the practice of Yoga Nidra. It is similar to the Plum Village practice of Deep Relaxation, in that it not only helps to relax but also to release deeply held tension and trauma. I believe this practice has helped to heal some of the deepest parts of my soul and psyche. I've been practicing it here at Deer Park. Every afternoon during rest time, I take my yoga mat and climb up the steep winding path, past the small stupa halfway up the mountain, and up to the very top plateau, where a huge white stone Buddha sits, peacefully looking out over the valley.

I try to find a shady place away from the hot sun and lie down on my yoga mat in the yogic posture of savasana, or corpse pose. Most people don't realize that savasana is not just a posture of relaxation, but rather a posture of learning to "die before we die." As we surrender back to the earth, we die to the idea of a separate self, so we can feel our oneness and inter-being. Slowly scanning my body, I can feel myself dissolving deeper and deeper through the "maya koshas" or layers of consciousness. Sometimes I float somewhere between being awake and a soft dreamscape, where images arise and dissolve like clouds. Other times I completely fall asleep, then awaken to find vultures circling to see whether I might be a tasty morsel they can swoop down and eat. Yet a part of me stays awake. Something is moving deep in my being without my even being aware, as I gaze into the vast blue sky above me.

Yoga Nidra has healed me in ways, conscious and unconscious. I used this practice while my mother was dying in palliative care. Almost every night I would come home after spending the day by her bedside, and lie on my yoga mat or bed, and breathe, and send love all through my body. Sometimes I would fall asleep exhausted. Other times, I could feel the places in me that were bracing against the pain I was witnessing in my mother's eyes as the cancer relentlessly took her body. I could feel the little girl in me who was desperately afraid of losing her mother.

Yet those years of cultivating an intimate, loving relationship with my own body and breath allowed me to hold this little girl, her tears gently pooling in the corners of my eyes. So I could go back the next day, and simply sit and hold my mother's hand once more, listen to her pain both spoken and unspoken.

Yesterday, as I laid here in this desert-like landscape with the vast sky above, the white statue of the Buddha as my witness, and the monastery in the distance, it came to me that I had already started my grieving before my mother took her last breath. Every time I lay down on my mat, it was my way of holding and embracing my little girl self. My grieving could be felt and released little by little, as a continual process that started well before she died, as she died, and afterwards through memories and stories of her life.

Perhaps I am also learning to embrace the little girl in my mother, who lost her father at the tender age of two, and who lay in bed listening to the sobs that racked my grandmother's body. Perhaps that's how we heal generational suffering, by simply learning how to breathe and embrace our own sweet bodies and feelings exactly as they are, knowing they contain the DNA of our ancestors and the dust of a distant star. We can trust those memories to arise exactly when they need to in order to be healed, just as I can trust the slow trickle of tears.

This morning in your dharma talk, you talked about transforming our suffering. If we listen to our suffering, understanding of that suffering along with its roots will naturally arise, along with compassion. As confirmation that I had somehow answered the question of my own heart, you turned and smiled at me and said "When you know how to suffer, you suffer much less!" As I looked into your eyes once more, I remembered one of the silent phrases imprinted on my mind in that magical moment in Vancouver. "You can be with suffering, and not be overwhelmed." Can I finally receive this blessing fully for myself? Can I now become a compassionate vessel large enough to hold the tears of the world?

CHAPTER 18

An All-Encompassing View

*The teachings of the Buddha are offered not as views or notions
for us to grasp at, but as instruments of practice. If we get caught
in views and notions, we lose the true teachings.*
Thich Nhat Hanh, *Awakening of the Heart*

I Can't See the Forest for the Trees

October 14

Dear Thay,

Today we got up very early for a hike up the mountain to Vulture Peak.
You talk about the Buddha and Vulture Peak in your dharma talks.
Vulture Peak in India is said to be one of the Buddha's favourite places
to retreat with his disciples, and the place he gave both the Heart Sutra
and Lotus Sutra. It must be a very holy place. I'm filled with anticipation
of seeing Vulture Peak here at Deer Park.

The sun is not up yet, so we've started out walking in the dark. A few
stars still twinkle in the night sky that will soon give way to the sliver of
light on the horizon. There are over a thousand of us at this retreat, all
walking quietly and mindfully in the cool freshness of this early morning.
There are people of all ages and cultures, some holding hands, all of us
walking peacefully together. As we take slow, mindful steps, we have
become one organism, like a snake slowly winding our way back and
forth, following the zigzag rocky path up the mountain. A few people
are holding flashlights, and I can see tiny pinpricks of light sparkling all
the way up the side of the mountain. As the path gets steeper and we
have to stoop and climb, I wonder if you are with us or not. How could
you possibly climb this rugged terrain?

Perfectly timed, we finally arrive at what I think is the top, just as the sun starts to peak up over the horizon. A few people are sitting off to one side on the smooth slate rocks, peacefully eating their breakfast. I sit down beside them with a sigh. I remember that back home in Canada, today is Thanksgiving, a time to remember the bounty and blessings of our country and the year's harvest. I look around at the beauty of this rugged landscape, and feel the sangha sitting around me. My heart is filled with gratitude as I eagerly open the brown bag that contains a light breakfast. The orange seems to taste especially sweet this morning, and I remember that even the simple act of eating an orange can be a meditation. Feeling the warmth of the sun on my skin, I am filled with a sense of deep contentment. I finish my breakfast, then close my eyes and sit in deep meditation, sinking inwards to the tender space that has opened in my heart with you, dear Thay.

I'm not sure how long I sat there, but all of a sudden there is a flurry of activity, and I watch as the sangha slowly snakes its way back down the mountain. The girl sitting beside me whispers that Thay and the monastics had just passed by. I am taken completely by surprise, as I had not realized you were up on the mountain with us. I start judging myself for not being more aware of your physical presence. There seems to be some kind of message in that. What else am I missing with my eyes closed? What other assumptions am I making that are wrong? Once more, with the full light of day now lighting up what had previously been in shadow, I realize there was an incredible view of the entire valley on the other side I had completely missed. Could it be that I'm not able to see the full range of the teachings, because I'm too focused on the teacher?

Instead of following the rest of the sangha, I scramble over rocks, before stopping to take in the breathtaking view of the valley and the mountain range beyond. There are still a few people sitting or meditating on some of the many rock slabs that dot the side of the mountain. A young lean man with a beard and long hair flowing in the wind stands perfectly still on one leg, balancing in Tree Pose.

As I sit with the granite stillness of the mountain beneath me, a feeling of inexpressible joy overtakes me. I have an image of you sitting peacefully here, in a country that caused so much death and devastation to your own homeland of Vietnam half a century ago. Surrounded by Americans who at one time might have been your enemy but have now become your friends and students, you have chosen to transform your own pain and suffering into peace and healing for all. I feel your exile from your own home, but I also feel your joy in a future that would not have been possible had you remained in Vietnam. I too am part of that future, part of that flow. "Peace is every step," I think to myself, as I begin to find my way down the mountain.

How Do I Live This Love?

Great love is both very attached ("passionate") and yet very detached at the same time. It is love but not addiction.
Richard Rohr, *"Great Love", Daily Meditations, July 23, 2020*

October 15
Dear Thay,
Today's dharma talk is a question and answer session. Another question has been slowly forming in my mind and heart, and I'm not sure whether I can put it into words, let alone ask it in front of the thousand-plus people here. Part of me wants to sit in the chair across from you on stage and declare my deep love and devotion in front of everyone. The other part of me is too shy and nervous, not sure whether I could even utter a single word while gazing in your eyes. While I know the familiar sound of your voice, I realize that you have never heard the sound of mine. Our communication is beyond words and sound, so you probably already know the question. Yet something in me wants to be heard. I decide to take time to write my question on a piece of paper:
I am deeply in love with my teacher. He is a deep bell of mindfulness

for me. His heart of compassion is boundless. I think about him all the
time. Sometimes I wonder if I am a bit too attached to him. He is my
heart's desire, and this desire has given me a lot of energy for my life
and practice. How can I live out and express this deep gift of love that
he has given me, without being too attached?

As the room slowly fills up, I sit with the paper for a moment, imagining what it would be like to sit directly in front of you and look into your eyes once more. I desperately want to voice my love, but I am afraid. Perhaps a part of me still wants to hide. I slowly fold the piece of paper, and slip it into my pocket. I'll wait and see f that same energy that catapulted me off my cushion in Vancouver gives me a nudge.

My cushion is about five rows back. A few people are talking and socializing around me. I adjust my cushion and sit still, starting to settle into myself and my own breath, listening from the inside out. The room is abuzz with conversation, so it is a relief when the large bell is invited, and the hall finally settles into silence. Once you enter, and sit, I am right in your line of vision. Once more I relive the memory of gazing into your Buddha eyes at the retreat in Vancouver, and my initiation into a vast love that knows no bounds.

A few people have gathered up on stage to ask their questions. The first young man tells you that his father had recently died of cancer, and he asks you how he can stay connected. Looking out at the whole sangha, you say "Your father is in you. I always invite my mother and my father to walk with me. I am walking for them because they never had the chance." Once more I sense that something more is being transmitted, not just to this earnest young man, but to all of us. The young man then asks about becoming a monastic, and with a knowing smile you invite him to come to the Winter Retreat, a chance to practice with the monastics for three full months. It seems another heart has been awakened!

A shy teenage girl then asked about feeling unsure and insecure in herself. This time, looking directly at her with that loving gaze that disarms and dissolves all boundaries, you told her to have faith in herself, that everyone has their own way of coming to the path. In that moment, I believe you transmitted something directly to her heart. As the girl stepped down from the stage, her eyes sparkled like diamonds. I knew the message had been received beyond words. Somehow it seems that everyone one of us receives exactly what we need, when our hearts are open and our minds are free.

The Christ in Me Weeps

Christ has no body now on earth but yours, no hands but yours, no feet but yours. Yours are the eyes through which he is to look out Christ's compassion to the world.
St. Teresa of Avila

October 16
Dear Thay,
This is my fourth retreat with you, practicing in the Plum Village tradition, and at each retreat I find myself settling into the rhythm and flow of the community practicing together. All the teachings and practices are slowly seeping into my body and mind, becoming a habit that naturally expands into my daily life when I get home. These practices give me a confidence that allows me to be a little bit more "me."

I find myself willing to be more vulnerable in my sharing time during the smaller dharma family groups. Our group usually sits just outside the dining area, in a shady space overlooking the road that leads up to the monastery. It's amazing how people who are strangers can connect and become close enough to share aspects of their personal lives during the space of just five days of sitting, and walking, and breathing together on retreat.

When I first started attending these retreats I was quiet about my Christian background, and most especially about being an ordained minister. I wasn't embarrassed about my Christian roots, but people do tend to stereotype Christians. When I looked deeply, I saw I held fear around being judged and not fully seen and understood. My inter-spiritual heart was still a tiny bud, not ready to fully blossom yet.

Even though you have written several books such as *Living Buddha, Living Christ* that weave together the teachings of Buddhism and Christianity so beautifully, Christianity has a poor reputation in Buddhist circles. I've met a lot of lapsed Catholics and recovering Christians at Plum Village retreats. They have left the ancestral religion of their childhood for many reasons. Perhaps the tired sermons and homilies no longer speak to the depth of yearning in their spiritual hearts or the gifts they want to offer to the world. Maybe they've been confined or hurt by out dated policies and doctrines that are squeezing the life out of once life-giving scriptures and sacraments. Some have been hurt and abused by the very priest or minister who was entrusted with keeping them safe. I feel the Christ weeping outside the church that bears His name.

People tend to put Christianity, or any religion, into a box of their own experience and understanding, especially with the "Christian right" being so outspoken on so many divisive issues: abortion, immigration policies, racial and sexual discrimination, and even climate change. When Christianity is put in a box, it feels like when I share from my own Christian experience, that I am also put in a box. A small rigid box is a very uncomfortable place to be. There's no space to move or breathe. I've been afraid of being judged, of continually explaining "But I'm not that kind of Christian!" I don't fit under other people's labels.

However, here at Deer Park I've begun to find my voice and reveal the Christ that lives and breathes in me, side by side with the Buddha. I've begun to share both one-on-one and in my dharma family group the truth of my own understandings. I've shared the mysterious connection I feel to both the Christ of my root religion and the Buddha who now feels like an intimate friend. I've shared my sorrow at how institutionalized Christianity has used rigid belief structures and power for its own economic and political gain. I've shared the deep sorrow and confusion in my soul for the senseless abuse of so many innocent people by a church meant to be a place of sanctuary, safety, and healing. Coming from Canada, I am aware of the traumatic effects on Indigenous peoples from residential schools that tore young children from their homes, stripping them of their language and culture, while subjecting them to abuse and bullying by those who were entrusted with the care of their young bodies and souls.

Now, I'm not afraid to share about the Christ in my own heart. When I share honestly, people often open up to me, uncovering their stories of being wounded and abused by their Christian religion. My roommate, Maria, shared about coming from a Catholic background and being a very "good" girl, growing up in Chile, faithfully taking her First Communion followed by Confession and Confirmation. With tears glistening in her eyes, she shared that two years ago her precious eight-year-old son died of bone cancer. When her priest came to visit after the death, he told the family that since the boy hadn't been given the sacrament of last rites, he was in purgatory, not paradise. At a time when this priest should have brought comfort and peace, he caused deep distress for Maria and her family. She was told that her innocent son was stuck in a holding place, not fit for heaven. With tears streaming down her face, she said "I still love Jesus in my heart. I just can't go to his church anymore."

This antiquated, rigid belief was causing her great suffering and pain, and so she left the church and found her way to you and this Buddhist community. I feel the Christ in me weeping for this senseless suffering imposed by a religious structure that seems to have lost its compassion and its very soul. Yet it wasn't exactly me weeping. There was no torrent of tears, just a soft and fragile crack in my heart that opened to a two-thousand year span of grief for all the ways that Christ has been crucified over and over again, and for all the innocent souls who have suffered because his true teachings have been so twisted and misunderstood. Other people shared long-forgotten memories from their childhood faith, when they had felt the presence of the living Christ. Our sharing contained the seeds of connection and healing, a small bridge of hope. It's time to move beyond the boundaries of religious structures and stereotypes to a new expanded community that can hold us all.

Yet we still have to heal the wounds of our past before moving fully into the future. You always say that we have to go back and heal our spiritual roots, or we will never find true healing, even if we become Buddhist. We have to acknowledge and feel and name our suffering, not just cover it over with bandages of new beliefs and religion.

From listening to comments about Christians in this Buddhist community, I have begun to realize how many wounded Christians and Catholics are walking around disguised as Buddhists. I have heard many offhand comments about Christianity that reveal a deep mistrust and misunderstanding of a religion that had been left thirty or more years ago. People seem stuck in an idea of a religion frozen in a snapshot in their mind of the last experience they had of that church. A lot can change in thirty years. The jewels hidden and preserved within the hearts of Christian saints and mystics through the ages are starting to be uncovered, revealing tiny prisms of light to guide our way.

I always love to see the pictures of Christ on altars at Plum Village monasteries. You too have a deep love for both the Buddha and the Christ in your heart. Sadly, I don't think there are many Christians who would place both the Christ and the Buddha or their altar. Buddha and Christ sit side by side on my altar at home, and more importantly in the altar of my heart. Many Christians think they have a monopoly on Jesus, confining the living Christ to just one religion and one time in history. Dogmatically, they preach that "Jesus is the only way," not realizing that Jesus is the historical person who manifested the Christ that is known by many names. Many spiritual masters from Sufi and yogic traditions speak freely of the Cosmic Christ energy that penetrates the entire cosmos. Like you, they know that this energy of love is known by many names and cannot be confined to just one name. In his *Autobiography of a Yogi*, Paramahansa Yogananda tells many stories about encountering the Christ. This seems to be the essence of what Christ was teaching. Christ is not just some historical person who lived 2,000 years ago, but is waiting to be born anew in our hearts, just like the Buddha.

While a lot of Christian churches have indeed stayed frozen in time, clinging to out dated belief systems as their pews continue to empty out, there are many that have moved on to respond to the unique needs of our time and age, as an "emerging" church begins to shed two thousand years of shallow thinking and hypocrisy to reveal the mystery of the Cosmic Christ that lives at the heart of creation, yet is known by many names, and by no name at all. This is the Christ and the type of spiritual community I long and weep for, one that fully welcomes and honours the sacred thread of divine love that is beautifully woven through all traditions.

In your inter-faith conversation with Jesuit priest Daniel Berrigan, recorded in The Raft Is Not the Shore, you say to him "I think that when you decide to do something in order to become yourself, and your thinking and aspirations become one, you might find that you are quite alone. People will not understand; people will oppose you. A kind of loneliness, a real exile, settles in."[21] I stand with one foot in my Buddhist community and one foot in my Christian community. It is often a lonely place to be, as I am often not fully accepted or acknowledged by either community. Sometimes I feel misunderstood or maligned. Franciscan priest Richard Rohr says that many of us are feeling this isolation, living on the outer surface of our Christian communities as we continue to push the boundaries and break down barriers. Sadly, many people have left and given up on their churches all together. Yet perhaps they've thrown the baby out with the bathwater. There are precious jewels that have not gone down the drain, but that need the light of our awareness to be discovered anew.

There is a lot of talk about inter-faith dialogue these days. I feel we need to go deeper. Instead of just talking about beliefs and philosophy, we need to create inter-spiritual practices that will connect our hearts in the language of love that is beyond words and concepts. Standing with both feet firmly grounded in the roots of both Christian and Buddhist practice, I feel perfectly poised to be a bridge and continue to live into my name "Divine Oneness of the Heart."

CHAPTER 19

Love Letters Are Meant To Be Shared

Our stories are not only ours, they belong to our ancestors and our descendants.
Sister Dang Nghiem,
Healing: A Woman's Journey From Doctor to Nun

Our Stories Are Not Only Ours

October 27

Dear Thay,

My journals are slowly filling up with all the letters I've written over the past few years. I pour my heart onto the blank pages and patterns appear that were previously invisible to me. As I write the chaos of my most innermost thoughts and feelings, snippets of memories and thoughts from my past arise, and are woven into the present. There is an inner transformation taking place that is slowly being revealed word by word, breath by breath.

I know you'll never read all these letters hidden in my private journals. Yet, at some level it feels as if they are being received and heard at a mysterious level, beyond sound. There is a deep listening presence between us, even when we are apart. Of course you would say that there is no "listener," because we're really not separate. There is only the "listening." I am in you, and you are in me. Yet there is still a part of me that longs to have a real heart-to-heart conversation with you.

At Deer Park Monastery, I bought *Healing: A Woman's Journey from Doctor to Nun* by Sister Dang Nghiem. Her story about her difficult life and transformation of suffering is a living testament to your teachings on mindfulness and compassion, but what really touched me was the intimate loving relationship she has with you. I felt a kind of kindred spirit. She put into words so beautifully what my heart already knows to be true.

Sometimes this is such a lonely love affair. There is no one I can share these intimate feelings with without raising eyebrows or attracting a look of disbelief and dismissal. My heart longs for someone to share this with, someone who understands this love that transcends all boundaries. As a nun, Sister Dang has the "luxury" of living at Plum Village, with direct contact with you. I have to be content with occasional retreats, or reading your books, or listening to your dharma talks online. While I can feel you in my heart when we're apart, there is something very different about being in your physical presence, a soft intensity that is felt beyond the boundaries of my skin.

After a mystical experience on her way to visit you, Sister Dang describes an intimate moment of connection, where you seem to already know what she's just experienced.

When Thay saw me at the door, he asked me gently and casually "You come to do what?" He looked straight into my eyes. I looked straight into his eyes and smiled and kept smiling. He reached out his hand to place it on my temple and kissed my forehead. Ever so softly his lips touched my skin, and ever so softly he walked to the car...[22]

I can imagine the tenderness of that touch, that kiss. Still, I wonder what it would be like to meet you close up. I long to ask you the many questions of my heart (if I could only put them into words!) Yet somehow you already know the questions before the words are formed. If I listen deeply enough, perhaps I'll slowly live my way into the answers that are always beyond words. It's like Sister Dang says,

"This is my teacher. He doesn't need to say much to me, and I have no need to explain myself to him. I tell him everything and I feel no

reservation, shame or guilt. I know he knows me more deeply than I am capable of expressing myself in words."[23]

That's it exactly. How I wish I could have a personal conversation with Sister Dang. I think she would understand this secret love I have in my heart for you, my dear teacher.

I am not the only one who shares the intimate secrets of her soul. After Sister Dang wrote her first letter to you, you responded, "My child, continue to write more letters to me." You do love to receive letters from your students. Even in that moment before we met in Vancouver, you said "I hope that you will meet the hermit of your life. If you do, please write to Thay and tell him." And so I did. I didn't really expect to receive a reply, but a part of me wanted to know whether or not you'd received my letter.

Last fall I wrote again to share my personal journal entries and memories from the 21-Day Retreat. Once more, I was secretly hoping you'd find a way of acknowledging them. I wrote that letter in early October, just before I left for India and Nepal. Months later, in April of this year, out of the blue I received this email from Br. Phap Tu:

Dear Vickie, Greetings from Plum Village. We are very sorry that we lack brothers or sisters who have time to take care of this email, so I take over this responsibility for now. It was me who was taking care of this responsibility and passed it to another brother. Probably he did not have time to continue, so there are hundreds of emails that have not yet been read and replied to. Please forgive us for this unskillfulness. I will print out your memoir and give it to Thay. I hope he likes it.

Thanks to Brother Phap Tu, I think there's a good chance you actually received and read it. This thought gives me much joy, to imagine you reading the stories and insights I've received from your teachings and the deep love and gratitude I have for you. Yet perhaps it's not so much the words that are written, but rather the feelings and truths the words point to. It was the very last page of Sister Dang's book where I have found the encouragement to write my own memoir, the book that is slowly unfolding in these pages.

"When Thay received the rough draft of this book, Thay said 'All of our dharma teachers should also write books about their lives.' I hope that my brothers and sisters will do so."[24]

It feels as if this message is there for me. I am not a dharma teacher, but I believe we all have a story to tell. So, I have decided to publish these letters, sharing my questions, my feelings, my doubts, my fears, but most of all my love, for truly you are the great love of my life that penetrates to the very core of every other love and relationship in my life, including the intimacy of my love for my husband. They are not separate. It is the same love you had as a young monk for a pure and beautiful nun, now transformed into love for all your students and disciples. I hope that I too can begin to grow and transform this love I have for you into love for all people, all beings, and for our precious Mother Earth.

Trusting Thay, Trusting Myself

January 30, 2014

Dear Thay,

Today I was supposed to be at a retreat at Mountain Lamp in Washington State with dharma teachers Eileen Kiera and Sister Jewel. Yet here I sit at our kitchen table, watching the snow gently fall outside the window. I had flown out to Vancouver a few days early to visit with Lanette. The day I was supposed to drive down to Washington, I received an urgent call from Doug. His father's health was failing, and he was being placed in palliative care. Doug needed to fly to Toronto to be with his parents, so I needed to fly home to Lethbridge to be with Andrew and Brendan.

Since I had already set this time aside, I am taking a mini-retreat here at home, by myself, while the boys are at school. I'm still disappointed. I was looking forward to a more intimate retreat experience with some of your closest teachers. Eileen met you back in the eighties and received the lamp transmission to become a dharma teacher in 1990, and Sister Jewel was an ordained nun for fifteen years before leaving to pursue her studies and teaching beyond the monastery walls.

Although it's always so nourishing and enlivening to be in your presence, the larger retreats often feel a bit impersonal. I need a more intimate and silent setting for my inner work to unfold. I long to truly understand, and to make sense of these confusing sensual feelings I have for you. It's so easy to fall into doubt. I often wonder if I am just imagining the deep connection I have with you...the looks, the smiles, the words and phrases that seem meant especially for me, when I'm with you in retreat. That same sense of intimacy follows me home, and I feel the lingering essence of your love even when we are apart.

I have kept this secret space in my heart solely to myself. And yet, I also long to share my experience with someone who might truly understand. Perhaps that's why I blurted out my initial experience with you in my dharma sharing group back in Vancouver, or perhaps I was just so full of your love, I could not contain it. At any rate, I don't think I shared very skillfully or mindfully. I wonder what Sister Thoai thought. I wish I would have talked to her, but I was too blissed out from my encounter with you to string together any intelligible words.

The day after the Vancouver retreat I tried to share the essence of this experience with both Lanette and Lana, two of my closest heart friends. Once more the words seemed to bubble up from my heart in an incoherent stream of words that likely did not make sense. Yet it was the essence of the energy behind the words that was received into the sacredness of their listening hearts. Still, I don't think anyone can ever fully understand the depth and intimacy of being seen so completely and with such pure love, unless they've experienced such a transmission for themselves. It is a hallowed experience untainted by our usual thoughts and judgments. Did you feel this great love with your own teacher?

When I got home to Lethbridge, I waited for just the right moment to share the experience with my husband.

Doug is truly the love of my life, my kind, gentle, patient soul mate. The love we share is a very special bond that not many couples have. We are each other's shelter, or "home" as you would say in Vietnamese. Yes, we may get caught up in the busyness of our lives at times, but we always know how to take time to truly listen to each other.

Doug understood that something very deep and life altering had happened to me. He honored that, and because our love is so strong and trusting, he has made space for you in our relationship. I don't think many men could do that, or be so understanding. Some might even feel threatened. He continues to support me in so many ways; giving me the time I need to travel to retreats, and even accompanying me to the Educators Retreat in St. Catharines last summer. We are so very blessed. There is an intimacy and trust between us that allows me to fully explore and express this facet of myself. With Doug's usual sense of humour, he often refers to you as my "monk boyfriend!"

There have been other trusted friends and teachers I have tried to share this experience with who have not understood, and have even denied it. I shared it with two of my trusted yoga teachers, women I have studied with over the years, hoping they might understand and share their insight. Both are well-known, respected teachers here in North America, and to my surprise both expressed doubt as to whether you were actually looking at me! "Perhaps he was looking at someone behind you," one of them said.

No one can belittle, or take this experience away from me. I know deep in the very fibre of my being what I have experienced with you. That exquisite moment when our eyes first met was a visceral experience of love in every cell of my body that cannot be denied. Ever since, I have been basking in the afterglow of that love. Can one ever put such an experience into words? How does one integrate it into their life and understanding?

I've been trying to do that for almost three years now and I still don't understand the full nature of this mystical relationship. Sometimes I feel like I'm putting too much thought and energy into this experience, and that I need to stop dwelling on it. Another part of me knows that this moment is a defining moment of my life that continues to reveal layer after layer, as I patiently strip away the parts of me that conceal, doubt, and deny. I can learn everything I need to know by looking deeply at this one moment, this one relationship, because this moment, this relationship, contains all others. You are teaching me about "inter-being," not just with you but with everyone and everything. I am in you and you are in me. The part contains the whole.

It has become evident to me that both of these dear and respected yoga teachers have never experienced this kind of transmission from their teachers, or they would not have been so quick to dismiss mine. They would have understood at a completely different level what it means to receive a silent transmission from a spiritual master. So, I'm learning to trust my own experience. I'm also more careful and discerning about who I share this experience with. People can be judgmental and dismissive, or wonder why they haven't had such experiences themselves.

I too wonder "Why me? What was it you saw in me? What tiny seed in me was ready to be nourished by these teachings, these practices, and your all-encompassing love? How am I now called to live out this great love in the world?"

I wanted to go to this retreat with Eileen Kiera and Sister Jewel to share this life-changing experience of awakening with dharma teachers who have received the lamp transmission directly from you. I sense the sacredness of this relationship that is somehow beyond time and form, but I was hoping these respected dharma teachers could shed light on the nature of this teacher/disciple relationship. So here I sit, alone at home, trying to take some retreat time for myself, practicing some gentle yoga, sitting meditation, and walking meditation.

As I invite the bell, the sound vibrating through space reminds me to come home to myself, my own knowing, my own wisdom. I can trust my own experience. I can trust my practice. I can trust you. No one else can ever fully understand us. Words can never fully convey or describe this experience. It is ours alone, our secret, your gift of awakening to me to learn, to grow, to trust in small moments of enlightenment along the way. One step at a time. One breath at a time.

A Love Letter To My Breath

April, 2014

Dear Thay,

I have learned so much by simply paying attention to my breath. Yesterday I went for walking meditation following well-worn paths by the river that flows through our city. As my feet touched the earth, my breath naturally fell into the same rhythm as my steps. With a quiet sense of joy, I realized that I am in love with my breath! A smile brushed my lips. I feel as if this love affair has been growing in me since my very first breath as a newborn baby. It includes the first conscious breath I took in meditation, and will continue until I take my very last breath.

When I got home, I wrote a "Love Letter to My Breath" in my journal.

Dear Beloved Breath:

You are Life itself, seeded in me in the love and coupling of my mother and father, then sustained for nine months by my mother's breathing. In those crucial moments just after birth, she waited and watched for my first breath, then with a sigh, watched you arise, and finally cry out in this new fragile body. She felt your movement against her skin, the life breath within her, now birthed into being. Many years later, our roles were reversed, as I watched you leave the frail form of her body.

We pay so much attention to the first and last breath, but what about all the breaths in-between? I want to give you my full love and attention, so when you finally depart, I'll have lived and loved fully.

Who are you exactly, my dear breath of life? You seem to have no separate personality of your own. Like a chameleon, you take on the colours of my many moods and personality. You follow me wherever I go, shadowing my every thought and movement. You patiently wait for me to notice the rainbow of feelings you are pointing to. When I finally do pay attention, you quietly change and soften, embracing me in the warmth of this moment, exactly as it is.

When I am caught up in worry, you get forgotten amidst the myriad details of both past and future, until I hear my teacher within whisper "Breathe, my dear," and the things I thought so important, fade into the background. The problems I thought so unsolvable lose their shape and form, and a fresh perspective emerges from the chaos.

What happens to you when I'm angry? As my body contracts, you are held in a vice grip, until this trapped breath is released, ricocheting wildly against imagined enemies outside myself. Once more, my teacher's voice says "Breathe, my dear," and I look into the eyes of the "other." In those eyes, I see a part of myself unclaimed, unrecognized, and the next breath softens my face, my heart, my rigid stance. I feel you breathing me. I feel you breathing in the "other." I realize it is the same Breath breathing us both.

Where do you go when I am sad, my dear Breath? It's difficult to give you space, for fear of what that one breath might release—generations of sadness repressed and unfelt, my mother's unshed tears for a father she hardly knew, for a newborn she never held. Those tears live in my tissues, waiting for that single breath to be free of the past. "Breathe, my dear," the breeze whispers, as a tear of sadness becomes a tear of joy.

Where are you in moments of joy? So full, so free. Like a woman who's just given birth, you cannot be contained in the vessel of this body. Those moments of sweetness, like the trusting look on my baby's face as he fed from my breast, the sound of my husband's voice as he whispers his love, the feeling of the sun peeking in my window as my body moves in an ancient rhythm of sun salutations to honour the new day. In these exquisite moments, there is both the free movement of breath, but also a deep stillness, as if time has stopped, to savour this joy. "Breathe, my dear, you are this joy."

What is the breath of compassion in me? To feel another's sadness or grief, I allow you into the sacred space of my heart. There, in this vulnerable state, you dissolve all my defenses against feeling both my own pain and someone else's. You seem to know that the heart cannot be coerced, but simply given loving space. Somehow, as I watch for your movement in another person, I realize there are not two people breathing here. "Breathe, my dear. The One Breath is breathing us all through both sadness and joy."

Where do you go when I'm meditating? You are sometimes fast and choppy, sometimes slow and silky smooth, often somewhere in between. You reflect the myriad thoughts on my mind. Yet somehow, just the act of paying attention changes you, as if you have been waiting patiently for me all along. It's like sitting down to have tea with a dear friend whom I haven't seen in a long time. I want to sense every unformed word you have to say, every movement, every nuance. And you return that sense of deep communion, becoming like the Christ who knows me intimately and guides me patiently to the Christ within.

So I sit with you, my breath. Together we become still, cultivating an inner listening, as I embrace our intimate relationship. I follow you all the way to the end of my in-breath as my lungs fill with precious life energy, then all the way to the end of my out-breath, as my lungs and mind empty. As my body releases tension, my mind softens, smoothing out the rough edges of worry and doubt and whatever else I'm afraid of. Somehow, you mirror what's going on in me, slowing down as my thoughts slow down, revealing a dance of both movement and stillness woven together by the thread of our very being. As I follow that thread, I begin to touch the still point at the end of each breath, the turning point of the breath and the turning world. a space of shimmering stillness, with a vibrant aliveness all its own. This still point of vibrant aliveness beckons me like a lover, and I want to pause longer and longer, to feel your gentle embrace. As I linger in this still space, you move like waves in the ocean. I stay settled in the silence, comfortably ensconced in the invisible arms of love, in an intimate silent communion with all that is.

PART 5

A Flame Never Dies

*When I look into the person of a disciple, whether she is
a monastic or a lay person, I would like to see that my teaching
has only one aim – to transmit my insight, my freedom and
my joy to my disciples. If I look at her and I see these elements
in her eyes, I am very glad. I feel that I have done well
in transmitting the best that is in me.*
Thich Nhat Hanh, *Dharma Talk, August 22,
2001 at Deer Park Monastery*

CHAPTER 20

From Me to We to Sacred Community

21-DAY RETREAT: WHAT HAPPENS WHEN WE DIE?

JUNE 1 TO 21, 2014. PLUM VILLAGE, FRANCE

Returning to Plum Village

May 31

Dear Thay,

It's been exactly two years since I was here for the 21-Day Retreat in 2012, although it seems like only yesterday. My heart quickens as I anticipate being with you again. It's been a long journey to get here, both in physical time and in the context of my spiritual life. Now that I'm finally here, I find myself filled with second thoughts. What exactly am I doing? Sometimes, dear Thay, you seem so far away. I wonder if I'm just having this love affair with you in my own mind. Other times, you seem so close, so intimate, as if we share the same skin. How and why do you affect me so? It's been three years now since I met your unwavering gaze of love. Perhaps it will take a lifetime to fully understand what all was transmitted in that moment.

I arrive at Lower Hamlet, and I feel a subtle shift beginning to take place. A deep breath, and the words from your gatha come to mind. "I have arrived, I am home." The quiet earth beneath me seems to welcome my tired feet. My eyes take in the shape of the large temple bell outlined by the blue sky. My ears tune into the cooing of a mourning dove, accompanied by the chorus of frogs from the lotus pond. Yes, my heart feels at home here.

After waiting in line to register, I find out I will actually be staying in Middle Hamlet, a two km walk away. Disappointed, a feeling of irritation begins to rise. Remembering to breathe into it, I let out a long sigh. Oh well, at least I will get lots of walking meditation here in the beautiful French countryside! I feel the beginnings of a smile on my face, and the irritation gives way to gratitude.

Just for today there is a shuttle that will take us to Middle Hamlet, along with our mountain of luggage, but with the shuttle not leaving for another hour, I take time to wander through the forest behind the plum trees. Seeing a deer in the distance, I remember looking into the eyes of the deer at the Educators Retreat at Brock University. Once more I am reminded of you, and what it felt like to look into your eyes. The deer bounds off, as if to say "Catch me if you can!" I follow to where it was, and see two deer leaping joyfully through the bushes. I sit for a few minutes in meditation, letting the living silence of the forest enfold me.

Chance Encounters on Our Path

Let the Buddha sit tall and beautiful, dignified and noble...
Let the Buddha breathe freely, nourishing each and every cell
of your body.
Morning Meditation Gatha

June 2
Dear Thay,
Staying in Middle Hamlet, with all our meals and retreat activities taking place at Lower Hamlet, means we have to walk two kilometres back round trip every morning and evening. Even though we have to leave before 5:15 a.m. to arrive at the meditation hall for six, I'm beginning to really enjoy the walk early in the morning before the sun comes up. The brisk morning air wakes me up, and cs the night begins to give way to first light, I can sense the rows of plum trees waking up, and sunflowers getting ready to turn their faces to the sun. I can hear the sound of the morning chant, punctuated by the bong of the large temple bell. Attuned to your practices, I stop every time I hear the bell, then resume

my walking meditation. The bell continues many times, and I smile as I realize that if I keep stopping every time I hear the bell, I will never arrive in time for morning meditation! I continue to listen as I pick up the pace.

Sister Jina began her dharma talk this morning with the question, "What will you do for the next twenty-one days?" She encouraged us to be filled with gratitude for the many conditions that have come together allowing us to be here. I think about the flow of my life that has brought me to this moment, and I feel gratitude spilling through my body. These Buddhist teachings and practices have blended with all the other experiences of my life. I can savour it all; every step, every breath, every moment with you.

Sister Jina breaks the practice down into tiny manageable segments, encouraging us to create a mindful walking habit. With a chuckle she says "Maybe every time you take the path to the toilet, that can be your mindful walking meditation. If you forget, you have to start again!" I have my own walking path here between Middle Hamlet and Upper Hamlet, and I have a feeling it has much to teach me. Hopefully, I won't forget and have to go all the way back to the start!

After Sister Jina's dharma talk, we are invited to gather in a circle for tea and sharing. Somehow the conversation turns to stories of you, our dear teacher. One nun shares that when you leave Plum Village, you often say to those left behind, "If you hear a cuckoo, it's me." It seems to be your way of reminding us that you're always with us, and we just need to be mindful and pay attention.

One woman in our circle shared a story that intrigued me. I had never heard anyone else share a story similar to mine. She spoke of attending a previous retreat, and meeting you on the path to the washrooms. She was looking down at the ground, when just in time she looked up, and there you were! "When I looked in Thay's eyes," she said, "it's as if he knew everything I'd ever done, and every good thing I had the potential to do." She said she continued to feel a kind of "lightness" for the rest of the day.

Wow! I knew it. It's not just me. How many others have looked into your eyes and been seen to the depths of their souls? For so long I have kept this experience a secret in my heart. Yet part of me also yearns to talk to others who have had this kind of mystical experience as well. I hope I get a chance to talk with her later.

From Intimacy to Community

With practice, we allow God to enter into our heartbeat and our breathing, into our thoughts and emotions, into our hearing, seeing, touching, and tasting, and into every membrane of our body. It is by being awake to God in us that we can increasingly see God in the world around us."
Henri Nouwen,
Spiritual Direction: Wisdom for the Long Walk of Faith

June 3
Dear Thay,
Today we will finally travel to Upper Hamlet to hear your opening dharma talk. I join a long flowing river of people walking slowly along the winding French roads. When we reach the top of the hill, we are met by a stunning view of the valley, including rows of vineyards, a pristine lake, and horses grazing next to a well-cared-for chateaux and grounds. It feels like being part of a painting in a French postcard. As if we are already one organism, we turn right and follow the gravel road, towards Upper Hamlet. I feel anticipation in my heart, to see you again. I can't stop myself from rushing a bit so I can get a cushion close to the front of the meditation hall. I find a place on the far side, close to the white board, where you often write notes from your dharma talk. Although there is a steady hum of voices, I settle into meditation so my heart will be ready to greet my beloved teacher.

The room is bubbling over with our shared love and devotion. As you enter with your usual slow mindful steps, it seems like you are imprinting peace in our hearts with every step you take. We all stand, joining our hands and bowing in reverence to both the teacher outside, and the teacher within. I breathe softly, watching as you arrive at the centre of the stage, where your meditation cushion sits. I feel the preciousness of this moment, and the intimacy of my own breath.

As is the usual practice on the first day of retreat, the monastics chant to "Avalokiteshvara," the bodhisattva of love and compassion. With eyes that are radiant with love and compassion, you invite us to allow ourselves to be enfolded by the collective energy of this worldwide sangha of over twelve hundred people gathered. Gently, you say "It's okay to cry. Feel your suffering." My heart is tender and open, but I can't really say what I'm feeling is solely my own suffering. It's more like a shared suffering, when we allow ourselves to be open and vulnerable to one another. Memories of some of the people I love and their suffering comes to my mind: the tremor of Parkinson's disease in my father-in-law's hands, the years of anxiety and pain he endured before passing away earlier this year; the deterioration of my Aunt Jean's mind, as dementia changed her from a kind mother and woman of faith to a wild woman lashing out at staff and family trying to help her; and, always, the pain-filled look in my mother's eyes as she lay dying.

The sacred chanting is so soft and tender. A violin and cello accompany the voices of the monks and nuns. The sound of the chanting reaches deep inside each one of us. The young Asian man beside me is quietly sobbing, and I gently hand him a tissue, a small act of kindness as we sit together as a sangha, embracing our shared humanity and suffering. Our hearts are wide open to receive your dharma talk on the connection between happiness and suffering.

After lunch today, I was sitting under the bell tower and started chatting with a woman from California. Out of the blue, she shared about an experience during walking meditation with you.

As is your usual practice, you had stopped to sit and listen in the middle of the forest, surrounded by the sangha. A large man stood up and started taking pictures, blocking people's view and interrupting the moment. She thought this was very rude, and started feeling irritated. She turned back to you, and as she met your gaze, the irritation dissolved, and an indescribable feeling of love filled her whole being.

I smile at her with complete understanding. Once more, someone else has put into words what I have felt in my heart, with you. I share a bit about my own experience, and a connection blossoms between us. We look into each other's eyes, only to find you, Thay, gazing back at us. In silence we share a profound understanding.

It's been lonely keeping this experience all to myself. Now I'm beginning to realize that many others here have also had these experiences of vast and unexplainable love with you. In our dharma sharing in our family groups, so many people expressed how happy they are to see you. Their eyes shine brightly as they share their stories of being back in your presence. One woman shared how she not only sees you in all the monks and nuns, but that she also looks for you in all of us.

I find this sentiment so beautiful. Perhaps I have been too self-focused. It seems like I'm only thinking about myself. "Is Thay looking at me? Is he speaking to me?" What I feel is so intimate, yet at the same time I'm beginning to experience a more communal sense of you and your love. Perhaps I am tuning into the river of your love that flows through all of our hearts and the heart of the sangha. Can I live both with this intimacy and with sharing your love in community? Is this what inter-being is?

Something is beginning to shift and change. I need to relax, and let go of holding you so tightly, so we can all breathe together.

Many Bodies, Many Lives

Our body is a masterpiece of the cosmos. Our body carries within it the stars, the moon, the universe, and the presence of all our ancestors.
Thich Nhat Hanh, *The Art of Living*

June 5

Dear Thay,

Today in your dharma talk you smiled and told us we have eight bodies! As a Zen master, you are always trying to dismantle our usual way of thinking. Saying we have eight bodies seems to be a Buddhist way of saying we are not just our physical body, and helps us expand our ideas of who we are. It's like a koan. It doesn't make sense to our rational mind, but can only be intuited by direct experience.

I usually don't take notes during your dharma talks. I try to just relax and breathe and be present to what's being transmitted, both in and beyond words. However, the idea of these eight bodies is fascinating, and I want to write them down. Here's what I wrote: (I hope I got it right).

1. **The Human Body:** the physical body most of us are familiar with. You also called this the wave body because it's like a wave of the ocean. It is the body that is born and lives for a short time, then dies and returns, to become the ocean.

2. **The Dharma Body:** the body of spiritual practice, is a kind of energy that arises when we come back to our breath to be present and gain insight. It is all the precious teachings and spiritual practices that you have transmitted to us, interwoven with our life experience.

3. **The Buddha Body:** the body of awakening. It could be called the Christ body, or the Thay body, or that of any enlightened being. It is the energy and awakened presence of our teachers already present in us.

4. **The Sangha Body:** the body of community. Martin Luther King Jr. called it the "beloved community," a community of people who share the same aspiration and want to support each other. It's like the kind of energy that is generated when we come together to meditate, or sing, or chant, or help others.

5. **The Body Outside the Body:** the practice of being able to see the Buddha or the Christ and also our self in everyone and everything. You said "Every book I write becomes my body outside the body. I can enter a home in the form of one of my calligraphies." We can see that we are not confined to the physical body.

6. The Continuation Body: our sons, our daughters, our students, and all those whom we have influenced. It is also the energy of all of our thoughts, our words, our actions flowing out into the world, and carrying us into the future.

7. The Cosmic Body, or the Domain of All That Is: the same energy as stars, rivers, and trees. We are children of sunlight and stars, and all phenomena. Through the insight of interbeing, we can see that there are clouds, and mountains and rivers inside us. Our human body contains the entire cosmos.

8. The Ultimate Body, or God Body, or True Nature Body: the reality beyond all perceptions, the water beneath the waves, the transcending of all notions.

Although at some level, a part of me understands and can feel some of these different bodies, my mind struggles to make sense of it all. So, towards the end of your talk, I put aside my notebook, close my eyes and come back to my breath. Once more, it feels like something is being transmitted beyond words. I can trust in your Buddha body (and mine), in the dharma body, and the sangha body, the collective understanding growing in us all.

Is the Person We Fell in Love With Still There?

When we first fall in love, all we want to do is look the other person in the eyes and feel their presence close to us...Just looking into their eyes is enough to survive on.
Thich Nhat Hanh, *The Art of Living*

June 6
Dear Thay,
Today your dharma talk is in New Hamlet. As the large bus pulls up in front of the wrought iron fence, I am filled with a sense of déjà vu.

Memories of staying here two years ago come flooding back. I slowly walk the path to the meditation hall, savouring all the familiar sights and sounds, gazing past the bell tower to the long lines of plum trees and the gentle rising slopes behind. Once more I am home.

Our buses were late this morning, and with no spaces left to sit inside the meditation hall, I take a seat in front of the open windows. It's quite lovely here, outside. Speakers are set up on the patio, so we can all hear what's being said inside, while listening to the symphony of sounds coming from the lotus pond.

Gazing through the open window, I am surprised to find I have a perfect view of you, dear Thay. You are telling a story about a couple who had grown apart. Once upon a time, they'd been completely in love. In fact, they had written the most tender love letters to each other. "How wonderful it is to receive love letters from our beloved, waiting for the mailman, being disappointed when a letter doesn't come," you said, as your eyes sparkled brightly at me. It's as if you somehow know about all the love letters I've written you, safely hidden away in the privacy of my journals. Are you disappointed that I haven't sent my letters to you? Do Zen masters get disappointed? I had thought about writing you a real love letter while I'm here, and now it seems like you've given me extra encouragement.

You continue the story about the couple. Over the years their love had slowly faded. One day the man had to go away on another business trip, and as usual would be gone for a few days. The woman felt lonely and frustrated. While she was cleaning a closet, she came upon a box of their old love letters. She sat down right there, and as she began to read, her heart softened and she started falling back in love. Later, when her husband phoned, he sensed something different in her voice, and decided to come home right away.

Love has a way of healing our hearts. It needs no words. She sensed him before he even came up the stairs, and was right there to meet him, arms and heart wide open.

You pause, looking around the meditation hall, and ask us, "Is the person we fell in love with still there?" We all wait in that sweet silent space between words and breath and thought. You've given us another koan to plant like a seed in the depths of our hearts. The answer is not readily available, but will take time to ripen and grow. My heart is so soft and open as I listen, as if every syllable is being gently dropped into the space. It seems as if you are speaking and looking directly at me, yet I also have the feeling that every single person here feels the same way. It is the miracle and mystery of Zen mastery.

Later, after a short break for tea, we all gather around the bell tower to wait for walking meditation with you. Slowly and reverently, we follow you and other revered teachers from around the world, including a stunning woman dressed in flowing orange robes. I recognize her from Middle Hamlet. Swami Saraswati is from India, and this is her first retreat at Plum Village.

We wind our way through the rows of plum trees, then slowly ascend the steep hill above. As drops of perspiration run down my neck, I glance up at you, concerned for your health and how hot you must be in your long heavy robes. It's amazing how strong and agile you still seem at the ripe age of eighty-eight. Unperturbed, you take your time, stopping often to enjoy the view of the vineyards and rolling hills below. The whole valley seems to be smiling back.

Finally, at the top, you motion for us all to sit and enjoy the magnificent view together. Swami Saraswati sits close to you, her hands clasped in prayer, watching every move you make. I see her later at Middle Hamlet, where we share a few words. She says she believes you are a walking Buddha. She has that "touched by Thay" look in her eyes. I feel it reflected in my own.

Meeting Thay in Tim

June 7

Dear Thay,

Yesterday, I was walking the now-familiar path between Lower Hamlet and Middle Hamlet near dusk, enjoying the sounds of leaves rustling in the breeze, and the forest getting ready to sleep. A Vietnamese man was walking in front of me, and the way he carefully placed each step reminded me of you. I came up beside him, and he turned and smiled at me. My heart melted. Tim is originally from Vietnam but now lives in the Toronto area. A fellow Canadian, he told me that he has been a student of yours since the early eighties. When I heard this, I couldn't help but ply him with questions about what it was like to be with you then. Tim says that you came to visit Canada quite a few times in the eighties, then started spending most of your time in the United States for your North American tours.

As he began to share about being with you at smaller, more intimate retreats, it almost felt like I was talking directly to you. All of his mannerisms reminded me of you, from his kindness and gentleness, his soft way of speaking and his sense of humor, to his dazzling smile. It's as if he's absorbed a part of you into his being, by being your student for many years. His very being reflects a deep practice and a vibrant relationship with all life. As I looked into his clear eyes, I could see you, and I could also see myself.

After meditation this evening, once more I am enjoying this nightly walking meditation between the hamlets. Once more I see Tim ahead of me, this time walking hand-in-hand with his wife. As I watch them, an inexplicable feeling of joy and gratitude rises up; gratitude that I too have now joined this flowing river, and gratitude for your teachings that help me to recognize and enjoy this precious moment exactly as it is.

You're Already That Which You're Seeking

Are you caught in longing for something in the future?
What are you longing for?
You are already what you seek.
The wave already knows she is water.
Thich Nhat Hanh, *Dharma talk*

June 8

Dear Thay,

Today I am sitting directly behind you as you invite the large bell. I had to come very early to get this spot, so with lots of time to sit, I've been practicing pranayama and meditation. My mind and body feels especially light this morning. Sitting directly behind you, I can see the fine hair on the back of your neck. I can see the folds of the back of your ears. As I watch you breathe, I match my breath to yours. *Breathing in, I feel my teachers breath, breathing out I feel my own breath.* I feel an irresistible urge to reach out and touch you. I clasp my hands in my lap as a way of holding back from acting on that urge. I wonder what it would feel like to actually touch you, to feel into that calm and contained energy that simmers beneath the surface of your skin? Once more, I feel like the woman from the Bible, reaching out to touch the hem of Christ's robe. Even in the midst of the jostling crowd, Christ sensed her touch. I sense a slight movement of your head, as if you've tuned into my secret thoughts and the touch of my consciousness.

I watch as you invite the bell, softly touching the wand to the wide rim of the bell first, to awaken a half sound. As you draw your arm back again, it feels like it is my arm, my hand holding the wand, then following a slow arc as the wand makes full contact with the bell. A shimmer of vibration explodes throughout my body. Every single cell in my body is alive with the sound.

After the last sound of the bell fades back to silence, the monastics begin the morning chant, *I take refuge in the Buddha, the one who shows me the way.* I feel the Buddha's energy sparkling in me as they finish. As you rise from your cushion to make your way up onto the platform, there is a subtle shift in energy. It's not as strong as being physically right behind you, but I still feel the intimacy of breathing together.

You begin your dharma talk this morning by inviting us to submit poems, music, and art to express the dharma and our practice. You glance over to me as if to say "What are you waiting for?" All right, beloved teacher, I will pour the passionate feelings of my heart onto the blank pages of my journal.

Later in your dharma talk, you spoke about how we often fall in love with a projection. We project our feelings, our longings, our hopes, our dreams, our craving onto the object of our love. You are now the stern Zen master, hitting me on the back with a stick to wake me up from my delusion. When we were sitting so close, could you feel my attachment and craving to touch you, to connect with you, to somehow make you mine? Am I so caught up in my perceptions of you that I am out of touch with the reality of you? Still, I cannot deny the intimate experiences I have with you.

How do I know the difference between my thoughts about you, and my lived experience of you? How do I allow the insights to arise naturally? Right on cue, in the middle of your dharma talk, you turn to me and say "When you are confused, go back to your breath." You smile lovingly. The stern Zen master is gone. I feel your breath in me once more.

Later, you talk about the Three Doors of Liberation: aimlessness (apranihita), signlessness (animitta), and emptiness (shunyata). When we enter these doors, we become more focused, and can become free from fear, confusion, and suffering. You start by talking about the practice of aimlessness: having nothing to do, nowhere to go, not having a goal, not even enlightenment. So often we are so focused on attaining a goal, of getting to where we're going, that we forget to enjoy the journey, and the scenery along the way.

At one point, looking directly at me again, holding my gaze with your penetrating eyes, you say, "Are you caught in longing for something in the future? What are you longing for? You are already what you seek. The wave already knows she is water." Wham! The Zen master's stick has found its mark. You know me so well. You know I need these wake up calls. I'm so focused on my longing for you, for God, for enlightenment, that sometimes I can't be open to what's right in front of, and already within, me.

Still, there's something about this holy desire and longing that keeps me practising and that powers my steps along this winding, twisting path. Your love is the spark that keeps the fire in me burning. Yet once the fire is burning, does it still need the spark? Many great saints and mystics, especially those in Christianity and Sufism, talk about their all-consuming love for God, for the Beloved, and how we must finally surrender and dissolve into that great universal Love. It is not only our human longing for God, but God's mutual longing for creation. In the Hadith Qudsi, God says "I was a hidden treasure and I longed to be known, so I created both worlds, the visible and the invisible, in order that My hidden treasure of generosity and loving kindness would be known." It seems there is a reciprocal longing between human beings and creation. I've felt that longing in your poetry and your deep love for Mother Earth, not as something separate from you, but as a part of you.

In *Dark Night of the Soul*, St. John of the Cross likens the transforming effects of mystical love to a log that is burning in three stages. At first there is the spark of ignition that awakens our yearning for God. This tiny spark begins to smoulder and smoke, burning away the moss and outer bark of the log, the self-imposed suffering and habits that prevent us from seeing our true nature. When the outer bark is burnt away, all at once, the log bursts into a roaring fire of desire that slowly consumes the wood. (Is this the all-consuming love I've been feeling?) Finally, the fire settles into softly burning embers, glowing from the light within, the tender love of Christ's compassion and love for all.

Perhaps it's time for me to settle into the softly glowing ember of my own heart. Can I let go of the fire and passion that originally ignited my heart, along with all the craving and expectation that comes with it? In the peacefulness of my own heart, undistracted by all the thinking and planning and craving for more, I can listen for the voice of the Buddha, the communion of Christ, the breath of my teacher breathing in me. As Fr. Richard Rohr says "What we seek is what we are, which is exactly why Jesus says we will find it...God is never an object to be found or possessed...but the One who shares your own deepest subjectivity— your 'self.' We normally called it our soul. Religion called it "the Divine indwelling."[25]

CHAPTER 21

Love Letters From the Universe

There are so many things I love –
Your eyes, the blue sky, your voice, the birds in the trees,
Your smile, and the butterflies on the flowers.
I learn each moment to be a better lover.
I learn each moment to discover my true love.
Thich Nhat Hanh, "Love Poem"
Call Me By My True Names

A Gatha and Poem for Thay

June 9

Dear Thay,

After your dharma talk yesterday, I wrote a new practice gatha for myself.

I'm already that which I'm seeking,
I'm already that which I'm longing for.
I am the water, not the wave. Be still and know that I am.

I've composed a simple tune, and find myself singing and humming it as I walk back and forth between Middle and Lower Hamlet. I vow to practice this mantra and see where it takes me. I will continue to breathe and yield, and soften, so I can let go of my wrong perceptions, of who I think I am, and continue to slowly live my way into the answers. There is no need to hurry. There is no need to rush. There is only the lotus that has already bloomed.

A Poem for Thay

A Reflection of Love
I'm already the water that gives life to the wave,
I'm already the lotus blooming out of the mud.

I'm already the tree in the soil of Mother Earth,
The smell of fresh bread in the prairie of grain.

I'm already the tea in a lazy white cloud,
My mother's fresh smile in the face of a flower.

I'm already the silence in the bell that's invited,
Already the answer to all of my questions.

I'm already the still point beyond every breath,
Already the exhale, my very last breath.

I'm already the eyes of love and compassion
Seeing beyond skin to the essence within.

I'm already the healing at the heart of our planet.
I'm already the peace at the end of a gun.

I'm already my teacher's wise words and vast heart,
Grounded in practice and shared with great love.

I'm already the Buddhist infused with God's spirit,
The Christian who's mindful of each sacred breath.

I'm already the cosmos, the ground of all being,
I'm already the one who has transcended religion.

I'm already the love in the midst of my longing.
I'm already the silence for which I am seeking,

I'm already the lover and also beloved
I am breath, I am life...a reflection of Love.

An Unguarded Moment

June 10

Dear Thay,

Today after your dharma talk, we practice walking meditation all the
way from Upper Hamlet down to Son Ha Temple. Walking reverently
through the towering pines, gazing down the hill at the throng of people,
I truly feel like we are all flowing like a river together. There is no rush, no
hurry, just the sound of leaves and twigs crackling under our feet, and
the silent listening of the forest. Finally, we arrive to the sound of classical
music from the courtyard, where we are greeted by the unlikely image
of a small string quartet—monks and nuns playing cellos and violins. The
sound is exquisite, as if I have entered one of the world's great concert
halls, yet the musicians are not wearing fine tuxedos, but simple brown
robes. The fruit of many years of meditation is apparent, as the purity of
sound is woven together with the pure love of their hearts. I sit with the
circle of listeners, and allow myself to feel the pluck of the strings in my
own heart.

This unlikely audience is filled with people from all over the world,
joined together not only in our love for music in this moment, but in our
love for you, our teacher, and this community. I watch as a small toddler,
not quite walking yet, explores the new-found strength in his legs, as his
father holds him, smiling his encouragement. I sit in rapt wonder as the
sounds of *Ave Maria* brings tears to my eyes. I feel the Christ child in
me being gently held in the loving arms of this Buddhist community. As I
glance over at you, I know the smile of child-like joy on your face as you

watch your beloved sons and daughters is reflected in my own.

Once the impromptu concert comes to a close, we are invited to eat the lunches we packed earlier this morning. I look into the bread, and I am reminded that this bread contains the sunshine, the rain, the earth, the care and love of the monks and nuns who have baked it. As I slowly put the bread in my mouth, it is as if I am partaking in Holy Communion, aware of the whole Cosmos, and my place in it. I touch life. I touch the Kingdom of God in this moment, and all moments.

After lunch, I decide to spend some time inside the temple. I open the door and bend down to take off my shoes before entering this sacred space. Just as I get one shoe off, there is a flurry of movement, and I see Sister Chân Không, leading the way, with you behind. I straighten up and step off to the side, bringing my palms together to honour my beloved teachers. I feel off balance with one shoe on and one shoe off. You look a bit tired after the morning's activities, and there is a far-away look in your eyes. Then, when you've almost passed by me, you turn, and your eyes light up, as if surprised to see me. You bring your own hands to your heart, and I feel your heart in mine. I feel like I have caught you in an unguarded moment. It is an unexpected, unscripted, ordinary, vulnerable moment of seeing and being seen.

A Love Letter From God

June 11

Dear Thay,

Yesterday in your dharma talk, you encouraged us to get in touch with the little girl or little boy in ourselves, by writing a letter to our younger self. I smiled at the thought of this, but decided to change it a bit and write a letter from God to my younger self. As the ink flowed, and words formed, it seemed indeed that it truly was a letter from God, or the One Breath that breathes us all. Perhaps we all need a letter from God.

Beloved Child of Mine:

You have been formed by the light of distant stars, part of an expansive cosmos that is both eternal and ever-changing, yet woven together by the fabric of Love. You too are part of th s eternal Oneness, coming and going, taking on form in the womb of your mother, then dissolving back into the silent Womb of creation.

This Womb of creation flows in and through all things, constantly moving and expanding into deeper and deeper expressions of Love. Know that you too contain all life—the knowing of a tree that changes throughout the seasons; the essence of a caterpillar transforming into a butterfly; the granite stillness of a mountain, and the flowing of the rivers and streams back to the ocean. All of this, as well as the knowledge and wisdom of your parents and spiritual teachers, and all those who have gone before, is imprinted in your DNA and consciousness, to create a unique being who is able to adapt and respond with love and compassion to the many challenges of living at this time on the earth.

Just as the very first breath was breathed into Adam and Eve, so too each living thing is animated and brought to life by this One Breath. This One Breath is the way back to wholeness for each and every one of us and for creation itself. The great saints and mystics have always known this. However, as civilization has grown and expanded, many have forgotten and lost this connection to the simplicity of coming back to the One that lives and breathes within all. Yet each of us contains the memory of this One Eternal Breath. It is the work of every one of us to remember this shared breath. It is learned and remembered in many different ways, in many different cultures and traditions, and through many different spiritual practices.

At some point in your life, when you are open and spiritually ready, I will plant the idea of "yoga" in your mind. Through this ancient, yet ever-fresh practice that has been transmitted through the ages by many great teachers and sages, you will discover and connect to this One Breath and the way of knowing that is beyond the cognitive and discursive mind. As you come into your own intimate relationship with this One Breath, you will be one of many vessels that will reach out and share the gift of this One Breath through the timeless practices of yoga and meditation. Many people will begin to awaken through the simple practice of becoming aware, that the great "I Am," that which many call "God," is experienced directly through this One Breath arising, sustaining, and dissolving back into the still Womb of creation. In so doing, they will be able to let go of their limited mindsets of who they think they are and who they think I Am, in order to surrender to the timeless and eternal nature of all life.

Your spiritual roots will be grounded firmly in the Community of Christ and you will be richly nourished and supported within the Christian tradition. However, there is also a part of you that will feel restless and constricted. You will feel a deep need and longing to grow beyond your own tradition and to find spiritual practices that will not only connect you to other spiritual traditions, but will ultimately point you back to the deep mystical truth at the heart of your own tradition. Through your connection to the One Breath, you will develop the capacity to be open to many diverse practices and beliefs, yet you will also be able to see the unity that lies at the heart of all spiritual traditions. With your deep desire for Oneness, you can become a bridge that not only spans and connects the distance between these religions, but that brings healing to lives that have become too busy to listen to their own hearts and to the hearts of others.

As you continue to deepen your relationship with this One Breath, and as you stay committed to the pathless path of yoga and other spiritual practices, this One Breath will guide you to an enlightened teacher, one who has fully realized the Pure Mind of Love through the simplicity of each breath and each step. In one timeless and unexpected moment, you will look into his eyes and see the eternal eyes of love, all of the Buddhas, all of the Christs, all of the enlightened beings looking back at you. In those eyes of love, you will come to see and experience the true nature of love that you already are. Like the woman in the Bible, touching the hem of Christ's garment, you too will be transformed in that moment and in the many moments to come, and in ways that you cannot even imagine. This experience will create a holy fire and passion in your heart. The Holy Spirit, the Boddhicitta, the mind of awakening, the desire to help all beings awaken to the wholeness and beauty of the One Breath, will become present in every cell of your body.

Yet know that these seeds of awakening will take time and practice to grow and come to fruition. Be patient, my dear. Know that there is nothing you have to do or make happen. Let go of your thoughts and plans and how you think things should be. Come back to the sacredness of each and every breath. Dwell in the quiet space between breaths, and I will dwell in you, so that each thought, each act of love and compassion, can arise from this sacred space. As you rest in simply being, you will be a blessing to numerous souls. Trust in my wisdom. Trust in the wisdom that flows through the One Breath connecting all creation.

The Silent Joy of a Butterfly

Silence is essential. We need silence, just as much as we need air, just as much as plants need light. If our minds are crowded with words and thoughts, there is no space for us.
Thich Nhat Hanh, *Silence*

June 13

Dear Thay,

As you undoubtedly know, large Plum Village retreats are not always very quiet! I guess with over a thousand people, it's difficult to maintain silence. I've noticed that a lot of people here seem to struggle with staying silent. We are social beings, so being in silence goes against the grain. I feel different from others that way. I think I have a hermit's heart. By the end of the first week here, I was longing for more silence. Something was calling me to go deeper, to see what lived beneath the surface of my everyday thoughts. I wondered what would happen if I committed to being completely silent for the next seven days. Would I go crazy? Who or what would I encounter in the silence beyond thought?

With some nervousness, I approached Sister Hoi Nghiem, the leader of our dharma family group, and asked if it would be all right if I stayed silent in our daily dharma family meetings. I explained that I wanted to spend a full week in complete silence. She looked at me with some surprise, but after questioning me about my practice to ensure that I was ready, she slowly nodded her head. Another sister suggested I make a name-tag to wear that said "Noble Silence," to let others know that I was observing silence, so they would know not to approach me in conversation.

I saw you glance at that tag the other day, during walking meditation. Can you feel the silent space deepening in me? Between us?

At first, staying in complete silence felt lonely, creating a sense of separation, especially at tea time, when people usually socialize and get to know each other. I watched people engaged in conversation--the smiles, the laughter, a hug here, a touch there, maybe a tear. I listened to the sounds of voices, catching words and phrases in different languages, sometimes loud, sometimes soft, sometimes more animated, sometimes just a gesture. I watched as faces revealed a multitude of feelings and emotions that are easily missed when we are busy talking.

Over the past week, I've noticed how much energy we spend in talking and constantly thinking about what we're going to say next. I've recognized the subtle details we usually miss when we are caught up in thoughts and words. All of my senses have come alive like never before. Everything is more vivid. The buzz of insects and the croaking of frogs at the lotus pond is an incredible symphony of sound, punctuated by moments of deep silence. The sound of the meditation bells seems to vibrate even deeper in my body. The light reflecting through the trees in the forest seems to dance and shimmer in ways I've never noticed. My bare feet delight in the feeling of the grass and the rich soil I walk on. The smell of freshly mown hay and the perfume of lavender carry the silence deeper into my being.

Silence is slowly revealing Herself, not as an absence of sound, but rather as a deeper feeling of aliveness. All of the natural sounds around me are intensified, while held in the sangha of silence.

I've been steeping in silence for almost a week now. Last night, I was sitting outside on the large wooden deck at Middle Hamlet. The sky was tinged with streaks of orange and pink as the sun slowly made its way under the waiting blanket of night. I felt a deep stillness in my soul, like the stillness you feel when you enter an old and ancient forest. As I was writing in my journal, a bright orange monarch butterfly swooped down and landed on my thigh. I stayed completely still, hardly daring to breathe as I watched it sense with its tiny antennae. What a precious moment. How often do butterflies land on people? I thought they liked flowers. Was this delicate creature somehow attracted to the sweetness of silence in me?

Even when I went back to writing, the butterfly kept fluttering around me, as if flirting and trying to regain my attention. Finally, I put down my pen, put away my journal and simply sat still and breathed. The butterfly fluttered a few more times, then softly landed back on my thigh. I let go of trying to do anything, and simply tuned into the butterfly exactly as it was. I'm not sure how long we sat there, just the butterfly and me. Time seemed to stand still. I began to feel a shimmering stillness not just inside me but all around me. It was if I could feel the quivering joy of the butterfly in my own being, in tune with the fragile beating of my own heart. Silence, as delicate as fluttering wings, had alighted in my soul, as words and thoughts dissolved. As the sun started to dip beneath the horizon, the butterfly gracefully fluttered away in ever-widening circles, slowly disappearing into the deepening shadows, as the silence of the night embraced the silence of this day.

Slowly, these words formed on the waiting pages of my journal:

Silence has settled like a butterfly in my soul. This lightness is a part of everything I am and do. It contains my deepest joy and my secret inner longings. I can always go back to this butterfly silence within. It is my birthright, my home, my lover. Yes, I love silence, just as much as I love butterflies. I crave silence in this noisy world. I can teach silence by being silence and listening to others in a world that constantly wants to talk about itself. I am silence. Perhaps silence is another word for Love. Silence speaks, often more powerfully than words.

What Happens When We Die?

How do I listen to others?
As if everyone were my master speaking to me
His cherished last words.
Hafiz, "How Do I Listen?"

June 20

Dear Thay,

Today, on the last day of this retreat, you begin your dharma talk by smiling broadly and saying, "This Twenty-One Day Retreat is a real treat." Yes indeed, it has been like a spoon full of warm honey slowly sliding down my throat. I can still feel the butterfly's quivering joy in my heart.

You begin with a mini dharma talk on how to invite the bell. As always, these practices are deceptively simple, but have layers of meaning if we really allow ourselves to listen. Holding up the small bell in front of your face, your delicate fingers gently cradle the bell, like a lotus blossom holding a dew drop. "Om Mani Padme Hum." The jewel of the lotus is in the heart.

You repeat the bell master's gatha: "Body, mind and speech as one, I send my heart out with the sound of this bell. May all who hear it, awaken from forgetfulness and be free." You touch the wand to the side of the bell and invite a half tone to "wake up the bell" (and us!) You then instruct us how to invite the bell with a balance of both power and gentleness three times. You look at us and say, "Listen with every cell in your body, because your ancestors are in your cells. They are listening too."

I can feel my mother listening in me. I feel my father listening in me.

I feel my children listening in me. Can we change the world simply by listening deeply? To this bell, to ourselves, to each other, to our planet? You remind us of the dream you had about a younger self being invited to the classroom of a distinguished professor. You say "I am no longer that young man. I have grown up. My life is my teaching." We've all grown up. We're all changing all the time. Just as our cells are continuing to die off and renew themselves, so too part of us is always dying and being reborn.

I too have grown up. I am no longer that shy, vulnerable, grief-stricken woman looking into the Buddhist master's eyes for a love outside herself. I have sat. I have walked. I have breathed into feelings of sadness and grief, judgment and self-worth, embarrassment, and feelings of not wanting to be seen. I have looked deeply at feelings of sensual spiritual devotional love for my teacher, feelings of attachment and detachment, of craving and desire, and all of the questions and koans that have no clear answer. I have embraced them all as part of myself, and am slowly growing into a Love that has no beginning or end.

"Nirvana is now, not after death. It's available in every moment, every breath." I hear you say. Yes, I have found a small spark of enlightenment perfectly reflected in my teacher's eyes, as I continue to grow into the Love that I already am. Somehow, you saw that back in Vancouver when you first held me in your gaze of unconditional love. You've held the mirror up, so I can see it in myself.

In your Zen-like way you say, "Birth and death 'inter-are.' Birth cannot be without death. The moment of death is also a moment of continuation. Birth is a continuation of the mother and father. Nirvana is to extinguish all concepts. No birth, no death. No being, no non-being. No coming, no going. No sameness, no otherness."

Then, looking at every single one of us, with your all-encompassing gaze of love, perhaps foreshadowing your knowledge of what was to come, you pour your words into your sangha, your beloved community:

I have transmitted my very best to you.

You have your Human body. Please keep it healthy.

You have your Buddha body, the seed of enlightenment.

You have your Dharma body, practice well.

You have your Sangha body. Build community. Support each other.

You have your Continuation body, your loving actions.

You have your Cosmic body, the stars and the trees.

You have your God body. Your true nature is timeless.

"What happens when we die?" you ask us. With that signature smile that lights all of us up from the inside out, you transmit the answer. " We don't die. I will be found in your breathing, your walking, your sitting."

Amen, I breathe. A feeling of gratitude completely envelops me, head to toe, from mind to heart, from me to you, to the whole world.

The Face of Satisfied Desire

If you make love with the Divine now, in the next
Life you will have the face of satisfied desire.
Kabir, "The Time Before Death"

June 21

Dear Thay,

I feel as if I have finally shed all the protective armouring around my heart. I can finally reveal and be the Love you saw when you first gazed in my eyes. This is a love that has no body, no bounds, no thoughts, no religion, no country, no me, no you. It is a love that transcends time and space, yet is grounded in compassionate love and service for all.

Some people might not think this a proper letter to send to a respected Zen master, but perhaps this letter is not for the Zen master. It's for the universal lover within that beckons to all of us to go beyond the usual rules, expectations and beliefs that keep us separate from each other, and separate from our beloved Mother Earth.

Dear Thay,

Our eyes met. The world stopped. No words, no thoughts, no judgment. Something long forgotten, dimly remembered—primal memory beyond words...a knowing...like the yearning contained in a seed planted deep in the moist dark soil of the earth—touched alive by your glance, your love, your fire, your passion breaking through the shell of my raw and grieving heart, to create the conditions for th s seed of love in me to slowly ripen in the light of your love.

No rules, no instructions, no expectations, no se f-consciousness, no need to shave my head, become Buddhist. Simply open to receive this love. Grow this love beyond boundaries of culture or religion, of you or me, of teacher or student. Be who I am, grow deep spiritual roots, go naked and dance, reach out and touch the hem of Christ's—or the Buddha's—garment, and be healed in an instant, as it ripples through time.

What is this love, this desire, you've awakened in me? A sensuous longing, a yearning for more. More of what? More love and compassion, more beauty and wholeness, an intimacy beyond words, an ecstatic union with all that is. You've lit a holy fire in my heart, a fire that's been quietly simmering since my childhood. With one breath, you ignited an all-consuming fire of holy longing for that mystical moment of union between lover and beloved.

Dazed and confused, often doubting, sometimes embarrassed, yet unable to deny this secret sensual love I feel in my heart. And yet, I know now that I'm not alone. Throughout all of history, the Divine Lover has been sowing seeds and making Love to everyone and everything, expressing that Love through a myriad of forms.

Rumi and Shams takes on new meaning for me. Rumi's sensual poetry becomes a lived experience, the touch of spirit on my skin, the Shakti kiss to the Guha cave of my heart. Of course I'm God-Intoxicated. Yes, I'm drunk on love. It's better than wine. I am that shy bride slipping out unnoticed for my rendezvous with the bridegroom, so the sacred marriage of all the seeming dualities in me can merge. I see the play of Lila, I hear Krishna playing his magic flute as the Radha in my heart dances to His eternal rhythm.

Never in my wildest dreams did I imagine spiritual love could be like this.

At first, I'm focused solely on your beautiful outer form as my teacher, like a bee drawn to honey, traveling to France, spending time in your presence, breathing in the fragrance of your love. The yearning continues, the anticipation builds, as I seek the intimate communion of love beyond form. This love grows in your silence, seeps into my skin, and a space opens up. It cannot be contained. Where will this all end?

"See me in all of my forms," you say. "You're already that which you're seeking." Yet, somehow it's not just the words that I need. Slowly, your love penetrates me at deeper and deeper levels, as the seed grows inexorably up out of the mud of my life. I begin to sense your steadiness in the trunk of this tree. I sense your touch in the caress of the breeze. I see your tender love in the eyes of a deer. I feel your joy in the silent quivering stillness of a butterfly. I feel your heart beating with mine.

This desire has blossomed into a sense of love and intimacy that goes beyond you, my dear teacher. This is what a love affair with the divine feels like. It's all around me at the same time that it's deep inside me. The sensuality and intimacy of making love somehow woven into every relationship, every tree, every blade of grass. The seduction of Spirit.

It's the return of the Mother, the Divine Feminine, arising from years of being smothered by out-dated patriarchal systems of religion and government that no longer work for the good and well-being of all. She seeks connection in everything, with a love that moves beyond race, religion or culture. She is already ripe and full in many of us, ready to give birth in an outpouring of reckless love.

This is the story of life, this divine love affair, an overwhelming desire, as natural as a flower opening to the sun, as powerful as that last push to give birth. I am my teacher's eyes, his ears, his hands, his voice. I am the Mother's eyes, her ears, her hands, her breasts. It's time to reclaim the sensual aspect of the Mother's love incarnate in all. It's time to give voice to the secret longing of my soul, for it speaks to the love-starved longing in our collective soul, for wholeness, for healing, for God in all Her myriad forms and formlessness.

With my eternal love and devotion,
Divine Oneness of the Heart

Afterword: Thay's Living Legacy

This is no ordinary love affair. I love somebody, and there's no one
there, just a white cloud, and an empty chair. It always was,
and it always will be.
Deva Premal and Miten, "White Cloud, White Swan",
Cosmic Connections Live

"With a deep mindful breath we announce to the world the news
that yesterday, the 11th of November 2014, Zen Master Thich Nhat
Hanh, experienced a severe brain haemorrhage. Thay is receiving
24 hour intensive care from specialist doctors, nurses and from his
monastic disciples."
Announcement from Plum Village, November 12, 2014.

With shock and sadness, I read these words about our beloved
teacher's stroke. Even as he lay in a coma, he continued to breathe
on his own, and those close to him sensed that he was relying on his
lifetime practice of deep awareness of breathing to guide his healing
process. Doctors were surprised at the consistent level of oxygen in
his blood, and said that it was a miracle that he was still alive. Thay's
students from all around the world were encouraged to "breathe for
Thay," and send him our healing energy. All of us were praying for
a miracle.

Weeks turned into months, and in April of 2015, Thay was
able to return to his home at Plum Village, where he could lie in
his hammock next to the creek, in the fresh cool of the bamboo
grove he'd planted more than thirty years ago. Despite being 89,
Thay made some remarkable progress, learning to eat solid food
again, but he was unable to regain the use of his legs, or his speech.
However, with his Zen spirit and focus, he was determined to do

everything possible to recover both.

On July 14, we were surprised to learn that Thay had flown to the west coast of the United States for an intensive rehabilitation program specifically adapted to his needs by world-class neurologists. Thay's diligence and determination were—are—a powerful message for all of us. Those closest to him said that he continues to be very alert and present. Although he made some small improvements, sadly, he was not able to regain either mobility or speech, and in January of 2016, he returned to Plum Village, where he continued to rehabilitate. He even appeared occasionally in his wheelchair for practices and ceremonies.

In April of 2016, I had the opportunity to attend a retreat at Deer Park Monastery in California. One of my roommates had just returned from Plum Village, and shared how Thay had come out in his wheelchair during walking meditation. In a forest grove, everyone stopped, and Thay made a point of turning his loving gaze on each person. Flora still had that "touched by Thay" sparkle in her eyes.

His flame continues to light up the world.

In October, 2019, Thich Nhat Hanh summoned his senior disciples to communicate his wish to return home to Vietnam. Two days later he flew from Thailand to Vietnam, communicating in a letter what it meant to finally come home: "Although I have lived many years abroad, every year when autumn comes, my heart always returns to the ancestral teachers of Tu Hieu Temple and I touch the earth before them...I wish to end my days in the home of my spiritual ancestors."

"Dear Beloved Community,
With a deep mindful breath, we announce the passing of our beloved teacher, Thay Nhat Hanh, at 01:30hrs on January 22, 2022 at Tù Hiêu Temple in Huê, Vietnam, at the age of 95."
Announcement From Plum Village, January 22, 2022.

I feel a deep sadness at the thought of our beloved teacher dying and leaving his body. I also know that I carry his great love in my heart. I try to express this love through every conscious breath I take, and every loving step on Mother Earth. We all continue our teacher beautifully into the future. I can't wait to see him in his new form! He always said that the next Buddha will be a community. Let's continue to build that beloved community.

Tomorrow I will continue to be, but you will have to be very attentive to see me. I will be a flower, or a leaf. I will be in these forms and I will say hello to you. If you are attentive enough, you will recognize me, and you may greet me. I will be very happy.
Thich Nhat Hanh, *Awakening of the Heart*[26]

NOTES

CHAPTER TWO

1   Full script for The Five Mindfulness Trainings is available on the Plum Village Website: plumvillage.org/mindfulness/the-5-mindfulness-trainings/.

CHAPTER THREE

2   Awakening the Heart Retreat, University of British Columbia, DVD: *Questions and Answers, A Deep Volition to Practice*, August 12, 2011 Plum Village Productions.

CHAPTER FOUR

3   Phillip Moffitt, "When the Student Is Ready" dharmawisdom.org/when-the-student-is-ready/

4   A gatha is a short practice poem, or words repeated out loud, or silently with the breath that calls us to the present moment. Thay has composed many gathas that can be used as a focus for our meditation, and as a way to help us be more mindful in our daily life. They are an important part of the Plum Village practice, and are used liberally throughout this book. I have adapted some of Thay's gathas to my own practice and life—another thing Thay often encourages us to do. You can find more information on Plum Village Gathas under Poems-Gathas at plumvillage.org/mindfulness/extended-practises/.

5   Thich Nhat Hanh, *Cultivating the Mind of Love* (Berkeley, CA: Parallax Press, 2008). 6.

CHAPTER FIVE

6   Sally Kempton, *Meditation for the Love of It* (Boulder, CO: Sounds True, 2011) 59-60.

CHAPTER SEVEN

7 Mark Nepo, *The Book of Awakening* (Newburyport, MA: Red Wheel/Weiser, 2011).

CHAPTER TEN

8 Thich Nhat Hanh, *The Blooming of A Lotus* (Boston, MA: Beacon Press, 2009) 37.

9 Swami Radha studied for a time with Swami Sivananda in India before moving to Canada, where she established the Yasodhara Ashram, in Kootenay Bay, BC in 1963. See www.yasodhara.org.

CHAPTER ELEVEN

10 Thich Nhat Hanh and Dr. Lilian Cheung, *Savor: Mindful Eating, Mindful Life* (New York: HarperOne, 2011) 50.

CHAPTER FOURTEEN

11 Thich Nhat Hanh, Dharma Talk, August 22, 2001, Deer Park Monastery.

12 Robert Munsch, *Love You Forever* (Willowdale, ON: Firefly Books, 1994).

13 Leonard Cohen, "Anthem," The Future, Columbia Records, 1992.

14 World Accord is a Canadian non-profit involved in international development, working with local partners on sustainable agriculture, economic and social empowerment of women, and strengthening the ability of communities to adapt to the climate crisis. See www.worldaccord.org.

CHAPTER FIFTEEN

15 Osho, *Tantric Transformation: When Love Meets Meditation* (New York: Osho Media International, 2012) 98.

16 Sally Kempton, *Meditation for the Love of It* (Boulder, CO: Sounds True, 2011) XV.

17 Ram Dass, with Rameshwar Das, *Be Love Now: The Path of the Heart* (New York: HarperOne, 2010) 212.

18 Thich Nhat Hanh, Review of *Be Love Now* by Ram Dass
(New York: HarperOne, 2010).

CHAPTER SIXTEEN
19 Thich Nhat Hanh, Dharma Talk, "The Tea Inside the
Calligraphy," August 14, 2013, Educator's Retreat,
Brock University, St. Catharines, ON.

CHAPTER SEVENTEEN
20 Henri Nouwen Society, Daily Meditations.
"We Love Because We Have Been Loved First." August 2020.

CHAPTER EIGHTEEN
21 Thich Nhat Hanh and Daniel Berrigan, *The Raft Is Not the
Shore: Conversations Toward A Buddhist-Christian Awareness*
(Maryknoll, NY: Orbis Books, 2009) 50.

CHAPTER NINETEEN
22 Sister Dang Nghiem, *Healing: A Woman's Journey from Doctor
to Nun* (Berkeley, CA: Parallax Press, 2010) 68.
23 Sister Dang Nghiem, 68.
24 Sister Dang Nghiem, 146.

CHAPTER TWENTY
25 Richard Rohr, *Immortal Diamond*
(San Francisco, CA: Jossey-Bass, Wiley, 2013)XII.

AFTERWORD
26 Thich Nhat Hanh, *Awakening of the Heart*
(Berkeley, CA: Parallax Press, 2012) 427.

Bibliography

Abhayananda, Swami. *Jnaneshwar: The Life and Works of the Celebrated Thirteenth-Century Indian Mystic-Poet.* Olympia, WA: Atma, 1989.

Boff, Leonardo. *Come, Holy Spirit: Inner Fire, Giver of Life, & Comforter of the Poor.* Maryknoll, NY: Orbis, 2015.

Chodron, Pema. *The Places That Scare You: A Guide to Fearlessness in Difficult Times.* Boston: Shambhala, 2001.

Das, Krishna. *Chants of A Lifetime: Searching For A Heart of Gold.* New York: Hay House, 2010.

Dass, Ram. With Rameshwar Das, *Be Love Now: The Path of the Heart.* New York: HarperOne, 2010.

Harvey, Andrew, and Erickson, Karuna. *Heart Yoga: The Sacred Marriage of Yoga and Mysticism.* Berkeley: North Atlantic Books, 2010.

Kabir. "The Time Before Death." In *The Kabir Book: Forty-Four of the Ecstatic Poems of Kabir.* Translated by Robert Bly. Boston: Beacon Press, 1977.

Kempton, Sally. *Meditation For the Love of It: Enjoying Your Own Deepest Experience.* Boulder, CO: Sounds True Publishing, 2011.

Khong, Sister Chan. *Learning True Love: Practicing Buddhism in a Time of War.* Berkeley: Parallax Press, 2007.

Lappé, Frances Moore. *Diet For A Small Planet.* New York: Ballantine Books, 1971.

Malachi, Tau. *Living Gnosis: A Practical Guide to Gnostic Christianity.* Woodbury, MN: Llewellyn, 2005.

Matousek, Mark. *Writing to Awaken: A Journey of Truth, Transformation & Self-Discovery.* Oakland, CA: New Harbinger Publications, Reveal Press, 2017.

McKay, Julie. *Glimpses of a Mystical Affair: Spiritual Experiences of Swami Sivananda Radha.* Kootenay Bay, BC: Timeless Books, 1996.

Munsch, Robert. *Love You Forever.* Willowdale, ON: Firefly Books, 1994.

Nepo, Mark. *The Book of Awakening: Having the Life You Want by Being Present To the Life You Have.* Boston: Red Wheel/Wieser, 2000.

Nghiem, Sister Dang. *Healing: A Woman's Journey from Doctor to Nun.* Berkeley: Parallax Press, 2010.

Nouwen, Henri, with Michael J. Christensen and Rebecca J. Laird. *Spiritual Direction: Wisdom for the Long Walk of Faith.* New York: Harper Collins, 2015.

Osho. *Tantric Transformation: When Love Meets Meditation.* New York: Osho Media International, 2012.

Rohr, Richard. *Immortal Diamond: The Search For Our True Self.* San Francisco: Jossey-Bass, Wiley, 2013.

Saint John of the Cross. *Dark Night of the Soul.* Translated by Mirabai Starr. New York: Penguin Putnam, Riverhead, 2002.

Teresa of Avila. *The Book of My Life.* Translated by Mirabai Starr. Boston: Shambhala Publications, New Seeds Books, 2007.

Tweedie, Irina. *Daughter of Fire: A Diary of a Spiritual Training with a Sufi Master.* Point Reyes, CA: The Golden Sufi Center, 1986, 2014.

Vaughan-Lee, Llewellyn. *Love Is A Fire.* Point Reyes: The Golden Sufi Center, 2013.

Vaughan-Lee, Llewellyn. *The Face Before I Was Born: A Spiritual Autobiography*. Point Reyes: The Golden Sufi Center, 1997, 2009.

Thich Nhat Hanh. "A Rose For Your Pocket." *A Lifetime of Peace: Essential Writings By and About Thich Nhat Hanh*. Edited by Jennifer Schwamm Willis. New York: Avalon, Marlowe and Company, 2003.

Thich Nhat Hanh. *At Home in the World. Stories and Essential Teachings from A Monk's Life*. Berkeley: Parallax Press, 2016.

Thich Nhat Hanh. *Awakening of the Heart: Essential Buddhist Sutras and Commentaries*. Berkeley: Parallax Press, 2012.

Thich Nhat Hanh. *Breathe! You Are Alive: Sutra on the Full Awareness of Breathing*. Berkeley: Parallax Press, 1996.

Thich Nhat Hanh. *Buddha Mind, Buddha Body: Walking Toward Enlightenment*. Berkeley: Parallax Press, 2007.

Thich Nhat Hanh. *Call Me By My True Names: The Collected Poems of Thich Nhat Hanh*. Berkeley: Parallax Press, 1999.

Thich Nhat Hanh and the Monks and Nuns of Plum Village. *Chanting From the Heart: Buddhist Ceremonies and Daily Practices*. Berkeley: Parallax Press, 2007.

Thich Nhat Hanh. *Cultivating the Mind of Love*. Berkeley: Parallax Press, 2008.

Thich Nhat Hanh. *Fidelity: How To Create A Loving Relationship That Lasts*. Berkeley: Parallax Press, 2011.

Thich Nhat Hanh. *Fragrant Palm Leaves: Journals 1962-1966*. New York: Penguin Putnam, Riverhead Books, 1999.

Thich Nhat Hanh. *For A Future To Be Possible: Buddhist Ethics for Everyday Life*. Berkeley: Parallax Press, 2015.

Thich Nhat Hanh and Katherine Weare. *Happy Teachers Change the World: A Guide For Cultivating Mindfulness in Education,* Berkeley: Parallax Press, 2017.

Thich Nhat Hanh. *Inside the Now: Lessons on Time.* Berkeley: Parallax Press, 2015.

Thich Nhat Hanh. *Living Buddha, Living Christ.* New York: Penguin Putnam, Riverhead Books, 1995.

Thich Nhat Hanh. *Nothing To Do, Nowhere To Go: Waking Up To Who You Are.* Berkeley: Parallax Press, 2007.

Thich Nhat Hanh and Dr. Lilian Cheung. *Savor: Mindful Eating, Mindful Life.* New York: HarperOne, 2011.

Thich Nhat Hanh, *Silence: The Power of Quiet In A World Full of Noise.* New York: Harper One, 2015.

Thich Nhat Hanh. *The Art of Living.* New York: Harper Collins, 2017.

Thich Nhat Hanh. *The Blooming of a Lotus.* Translated by Annabel Laity. Boston: Beacon Press, 2009.

Thich Nhat Hanh and Daniel Berrigan. *The Raft Is Not the Shore: Conversations Toward A Buddhist-Christian Awareness.* Maryknoll: Orbis, 1975, 2001.

 **VICKIE MACARTHUR** is passionate about building bridges and creating connections. Based in Western Canada, Vickie has been creating community through her yoga studio, Spirit in Motion Yoga, since 2001. Her teaching and writing integrate embodied awareness, breath, and spirituality, offering healing and wholeness to individuals and groups. As a minister and spiritual director, Vickie accompanies people of all faiths on their spiritual journey by honoring the depth of all traditions. Rooted in her Christian, Buddhist, and yoga communities, she works with the Lethbridge Interfaith Network, Creating Connection West, and with Awakening Spirituality to build bridges, and create new kinds of spiritual communities. Vickie is a frequent guest with Nurturing Spirit retreats on the West Coast and at the Martha Retreat Centre, near her home in Lethbridge, Alberta. She is a member of SDI International, Canadian Jubilee, and Spiritual Directors Lethbridge. With an inter-spiritual heart that sees beyond the surface, she invites others into that intimate space of communion with the perennial wisdom that flows through all spiritual traditions.

www.vickiemacarthur.com
www.spiritinmotionyoga.com

Manufactured by Amazon.ca
Bolton, ON